Calm Parents
CONFIDENT KIDS

How to Use Brain Training to Raise Happy Resilient Children

FOREWORD BY DANA WILDE

CONTRIBUTING AUTHORS
- Marion Solis • Renee Realta • Lee Collver-Richards
- Deborah C. Owen • Kristin A. Carbone
Patricia Dawn Clark • Tamara Jackson Clark
- Louisa Joy Dykstra • Murielle Fellous
- Constance Greer • Deborah Helser
- Angela Humburg • Michelle Lowbeer
- Charity Nicole

Calm Parents Confident Kids
Early Praises & Gratitude

"We are honored these fifteen authors have come together to recognize the Peace Academy of the Sciences and Arts and dedicate their proceeds to help us grow in our sphere of impact. Calm Parents, Confident Kids is perfectly aligned with Peace Academy's beliefs about children.

It uses our knowledge about brain science to guide us through powerful strategies that are conducive to parents' well-being and the healthy social-emotional development of their children. When we teach children to respect their brain signals from a young age, we are essentially supporting their formation of a positive self-perception which then translates to grit, perseverance, and intellectual flexibility as they grow into their teenage years. This makes them adept in interrupting negative thoughts perpetuated by their external experiences then, translating these thoughts into positive and meaningful shifts that are transformative to their development.

With easy-to-read examples and fun relatable stories, these authors ultimately show us how to teach children the skills

to responsibly control what they have control of while navigating the ups and downs of life.

Thank you for creating your work in honor of the Peace Academy!"

Noha Kolkailah, Founder & CEO, The Peace Academy of the Sciences and Arts (PASA) www.peaceacademyslo.org

"As an author, healer, teacher, actor, and pro-active activist in all things focused on love, I highly recommend the book *Calm Parents Confident Kids: How to Use Brain Training to Raise Happy Resilient Children* as another love song to the heroic human journey of living, loving, and creating consciously. An easy, simple read that has you knowing how to love yourself more and so, with loving tenderness and fierce compassion, how to model for the children in your care, how natural self-love really is. How deserving they are of knowing their own love. How much the world cherishes, honors, and supports them in their lives to live freely and create consciously. And, how important it is to develop an inner dialogue that promotes creativity, justice, innovation, and vibrant health. When you take charge of the thoughts you think, from the inside out, you become the Captain of your Ship, the author of a destiny filled with the love that You. Always. Are. And that my friends, is a wonderful place to

 begin a day, every day, in tune, mindful, aware, and honest about what is your own "*normal state*" and how magnificent life can be when you create your world from your truest, happiest "*angel of your higher nature*".

Dee Wallace, actor & author "Born: Giving Birth to a New You"
www.iamdeewallace.com

"Lee Collver-Richards comes into this necessary project like a comet in the literary scene. Her contribution to this book elevates the reader with her unique and high frequency way of expressing truth...you are going to get more than you realise from reading *Calm Parents Confident Kids.*"

Sandra and Daniel Biskind, spiritual leaders, global speakers, and the international #1 bestselling authors of *Codebreaker: Discover the Password to Unlock the Best Version of You* and its companion Codebreaker journal." <u>www.thebiskinds.com</u>

"This is a must-read for any parent of young kids, and for anyone who wants to get a better understanding of how powerful thoughts can be.

Knowing that one has a choice in what one chooses to think and focus on, and that a parent can help teach their child this precious life lesson is invaluable. Any parent would benefit from the learnings from this book as they navigate the wonderful yet unpredictable (and sometimes exhausting) adventure of parenthood.

It is amazing — and sometimes scary — to realize how one's childhood greatly influences one's future development. This book has so many different and varied insights — from modelling to mantras — how to make the parenting journey that much more enjoyable, and successful."

PY Nicole Chang, Harvard graduate, entrepreneur, high performance coach, author, owner of The Coder School Pasadena, and mother of two. https://www. thecoderschool.com/locations/pasadena/

"How can I adequately thank the creators of this profound book!?

What more beautiful gift to give another but awareness of their own perfection, emotionality, psychology, physiology, and power!? AND ability to be happy!? AND to pass this onto our children?

I believe, no, I know, we are born to be happy. Thanks for putting the power and happiness back in our own hands (and brains and bodies!)

The humanity, care and love expressed here and turned into helpful, hopeful, practical, reminders, guidance, support, and tools are a superb contribution to us as a society finding its way to love and affirmation. If we are to create (or continue to create) enriching lives for ourselves, families, and society, it's principles like these that light the way.

And yes, I know this book is written for parents.- and it is an articulate, easy to read and apply, diverse, kind guide for this .

And I personally am restored, enlivened, comforted, and reminded of all the good, love, support, beauty, creativity, and kindness in the world, and my and others capacity for this.

To the authors- if you women do nothing else in your lives (and I know this is impossible) you have gifted an immense gift. Thanks, from me, our children, and future generations."

Kindle Customer
5.0 out of 5 Stars
A Complete Gift!
Reviewed in Australia on March 23, 2022

"*Calm Parents Confident Kids* had me hooked right from the start! Originally, I sat down to read just a chapter, and before I knew it, I was more than halfway done with the book. As a mother of four myself, it is refreshing to hear other moms being transparent about what they have been through. Even better when each chapter then shows us easily how using the brain training techniques really help change parenting habits, leading to happier and healthier children. Personally, I am stoked to really dig in and learn more about these techniques. I am also very much going to keep this book handy to refer back to often! Highly recommend this fun, informative and easy to read book for everyone!"

Tara Davis
5.0 out of 5 stars
Incredibly Relatable and Informative (wiith no blue line)
Reviewed in the United States on March 23, 2022

A Blank Page is like a fresh breath. Full of all thought, all possibility, and infinite potential. From this new breath, seated in the One Mind and One Heart of Love, Create JOY.

With love and immense gratitude to you, dear reader…

Thank you!
The Authors

"It is hard to sneak a look at God's cards. But that He would choose to play dice with the world… is something I cannot believe for a single moment."

Albert Einstein in a letter to Cornelius Lanczos, March 21, 1942, AEA 15-294

This book is in honor of:

All the parents, children, teachers, and students past, present, and future, Thank You!

You make our world, and the planet we share, a healthier, happier, saner, more peaceful, creative place for everyone.

Proceeds of this work will be gifted to the continued success of two brilliant Palaces of Learning:

The Peace Academy of the Sciences and the Arts, California. PASA's mission is to inspire a deep understanding of self and others through a sovereign learning culture. PASA celebrates creative innovation, enriched collaborative experiences and connection through core human values by co-creating an evolving and fluid community of lifelong learners who become competent caretakers and peace leaders for our world. (www.peaceacademyslo.org)

And SSS Anand Van, Indara, India and the Anand Van schools, whose mission is to pave the way for Children and Communities to Anand Van by Nurturing and Empowering the Realization of their greatest and Highest Potential to be Future sovereign beings of Heaven on Earth as One World, One Love, One Heart, One Humanity.

(www.sssanandvan.com)

Calm Parents
CONFIDENT KIDS

How to Use Brain Training to Raise Happy Resilient Children

FOREWORD BY DANA WILDE

CONTRIBUTING AUTHORS
- Marion Solis • Renee Realta • Lee Collver-Richards
- Deborah C. Owen • Kristin A. Carbone
Patricia Dawn Clark • Tamara Jackson Clark
- Louisa Joy Dykstra • Murielle Fellous
- Constance Greer • Deborah Helser
- Angela Humburg • Michelle Lowbeer
- Charity Nicole

CALM PARENTS CONFIDENT KIDS:
HOW TO USE BRAIN TRAINING
TO RAISE HAPPY RESILIENT CHILDREN

Hummingbird Communications
A TELESIS COMPANY

Copyright © 2022 Hummingbird Communications

www.CalmParentsConfidentKids.com

First edition printed in 2022

Edited by Deborah C. Owen
Audible Read by Renee Realta
Cover design by Martha Vorel
Interior design by Amit Dey

Published by Spotlight Publishing.

Library of Congress catalog and card number: 2021924662

Paperback ISBN: 978-1-7338224-0-4
Hardcover ISBN 978-1-7338224-1-1
eBook ISBN 978-1-7338224-2-8
Audible ISBN 978-1-7338224-3-5

TABLE OF CONTENTS

"Until you make the unconscious conscious, it will direct your life and you will call it fate."

- Carl Jung, 1959

FOREWORD

By Dana Wilde

When I was 19 years old, I was working for a major American corporation. I started the cubicle job at the corporation the previous year, straight out of high school. While the job paid well enough, I forewent college to start working and soon found out that corporate life wasn't all I thought it would be.

Living inside a cubicle was stressful, and I was miserable in that position. I was so unhappy that I remember sitting in the parking lot during lunch hour, crying because I didn't want to go back inside and sit in that cubicle.

Then one day, salvation arrived. What saved me from that cubicle was an intensive 40-hour training on how the brain worked.

The program was called "Investments in Excellence," and the creator was Lou Tice. His program helped me understand how my thinking created my outcomes, and from that day forward, the whole world opened for me. I immediately quit the cubicle job and began what I started to call "my big adventure." In my mind, the big adventure is the adventure we're all on. It's the adventure called "life."

The information that I learned from Lou Tice allowed me to "train my brain" to live my life on my terms.

I became a published author at age twenty-three.

I lived overseas.

I worked in the film industry and won awards.

And I built two million-dollar businesses.

But the best benefit of training my brain is that I know how to stay emotionally aligned. I know how to be authentically, deeply happy.

Happiness is something that all of us have at our fingertips. We generate happiness by the thoughts we think, and each of us can become focused, proactive thinkers.

While I was building my first business, I was surprised to find that there wasn't much material available for entrepreneurs on the topic of positive mindset.

The lack of material inspired me to write my book, Train Your Brain. At the time, I published the material first as a live training and then as a CD Set. The demand grew, and the book soon followed.

In creating the *Train Your Brain* material, I had one goal. Teach other entrepreneurs how to build million-dollar businesses by leveraging the power of mindset. That was it.

Of course, I knew that if the entrepreneurs applied the *Train Your Brain* principles to other areas of their lives, they would get results in those areas too. We received emails and letters from fans who used *Train Your Brain* to lose weight, for PTSD, to find love, and to parent.

It was just a matter of time before people asked for a book about how parents could use *Train Your Brain* with their kids.

Entrepreneurs who initially followed the *Train Your Brain* material to grow their businesses were using these mindset principles with their kids, and they were hungry for more.

I could appreciate the request, but I knew that I was not the best person to write a parenting book. I don't have kids. I could never write a parenting book with the passion and firsthand experience of the parents using brain training with their kids.

As the adage says, "write what you know," and I knew that a book for parents was not on the agenda for me. To my surprise, the entrepreneur parents in the *Train Your Brain* "sandbox" collaborated, and the result is the book you hold in your hands.

The authors of this book are parents who have been using *Train Your Brain* philosophies to raise centered, happy children and to be happier and more centered themselves. As you turn the pages of this book, you will discover that this book is not only about instilling a better mindset in your children but also "training your own brain" too.

The best part of this book is that it far surpasses the original *Train Your Brain* philosophies because you get the combined experience of all the authors here. These authors have their own modalities and techniques woven into their parenting experience, alongside *Train Your Brain*.

You have in your hands a tome of wisdom that will inspire you and benefit your children. It's a book that couldn't have been created any other way.

Lou Tice passed the information to me.

I passed on what I learned.

The authors of this book have been teaching their children, and now they are passing it on to you. It makes me laugh to think that when I attended Lou Tice's training nearly forty years ago, my 19-year-old-self thought, "I wish I would have learned this information about mindset sooner."

The wisdom you garner here will be a gift to your children. It will also be a gift to yourself. Get ready to *Train Your Brain* and start your new adventure.

Dana Wilde
Menomonie, Wisconsin
September 23, 2021

PART ONE

I THINK, THEREFORE, I AM?

"Cogito, Ergo Sum"

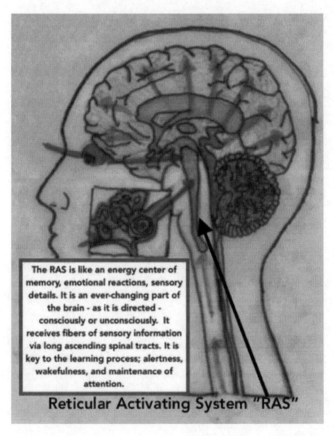

The RAS is like an energy center of memory, emotional reactions, sensory details. It is an ever-changing part of the brain - as it is directed - consciously or unconsciously. It receives fibers of sensory information via long ascending spinal tracts. It is key to the learning process; alertness, wakefulness, and maintenance of attention.

Reticular Activating System "RAS"

Figure 1: *The Human Brain's Reticular Activating System(RAS) by LACR*

INTRODUCTION

by Lee Collver-Richards

Congratulations! The book you have in your hands will send you on a journey of total freedom – the EASY way. Don't get us wrong, shifting our brain's programs out of lifetimes of conditioned beliefs is a task reserved for only the brave of heart, stalwart of mind, and present in body.

In other words, anyone who has ever been, or contemplates becoming, a parent, a leader, a teacher, a steward of new life.

As a parent, you are your child's best teacher, and they are yours. Each of us alternates between teacher and student throughout our entire lifetime. The process of growing and learning allows us to transform that sacred, intimate, ever-so-personal, and unique relationship with life itself.

Creating, investigating, imagining, innovating, playing, inquiring, and transforming are integral to healthy human life. As parents in the human family, it is our inimitable right to provide the foundations of a healthy life for our children. Even, or especially, if we never felt we had it available ourselves.

It is our hope to seed for you, Beloved Readers:

- How to model the power of conscious thinking for the children in your loving care.
- How to practice with them.
- How to celebrate every time they show you that they know and can consciously do for themselves.
- To heighten self-awareness and mindful guidance practices.
- To commune with the qualities of virtue as sovereign and interdependent human beings.
- To dissolve ignorance and live true bliss.
- To foster loving kindness in all relationships.
- To provide a variety of approaches and practices in how we can transform our brain's unconscious, fixed mindset.
- To shift our perspectives for the better and to our advantage.
- To develop mastery and true freedom of choice at every age and stage of our lives.

This book is for anyone who chooses to live as a responsible human being. For to operate optimally, the complex human mind requires ongoing direction, through conscious choice, in every waking moment. And calm, clear, consistent rest time to accomplish its natural rejuvenation processes.

Our physical health and wellness require the zero point or the constant rebalancing of homeostasis of all the body systems, on all four levels of being, in a constant dance of movement, rest, observing, and action:

- Mental body requires a clear, calm mind
- Physical body requires a pure body, full of nourishment, and gratitude
- Emotional body requires an open heart generating and practicing unconditional love
- Spiritual body requires a light spirit, joy, creativity, and connection

Your body's operating system is your brain. It supports all the body's natural functions for health and wellness. Most of what the body accomplishes naturally is done in the unseen realms – it is in the unconscious. We don't "think" to breathe. We don't effort to breathe. Yet we can limit or constrict our breath flow by "trying to control it" from a mind gone amok.

Directions from an undisciplined mind hamper learning, cut off potential, and squash creativity because the undisciplined, unconscious mind is like a rogue. Its directions are neither clear nor focused. Mental and emotional health imbalances can cause serious relationship instability and destroy trust. Trust is another quality essential to a healthy, happy life. Consciously retraining your mind to flow with your own and each other's natural creative genius is truly a necessity in these times.

Learning requires a quiet mind inside a relaxed nervous system. Learning also requires physical safety where others can meet you in relaxed mindfulness. Honoring and cultivating this sacred space of physical, mental, and emotional safety gives rise to creativity flow and harmonious relationships. It is free of judgments and builds confidence, self-esteem, and mental acuity.

The creation of physical safety and trust begin within a disciplined mind. It's a mind that knows how to work with all energy in respect, equanimity, wonder, and gratitude. When you cultivate and honor a growth mindset, you smile at negative fears (false evidence appearing real) and you meet new learning or the unknown, with trust, resilience, and wonder. You know how to defeat insecurity rather than feed it.

As Dawson Church so aptly wrote in "Mind to Matter"(2018), the human mind has at its beck and call an infinite myriad of possibilities for its entire lifetime. Foundational sciences, religion, education, and governance have heretofore ignored, or worse, denied, and hid.

Unfortunately, many children struggle to learn well in school. There may be times when internal worries have them believing the negative stories about their capacity or worth in their worlds. Or they may not feel physically safe. Labeling and categorizing a child as gifted or disabled, intelligent or dull, also contribute to the struggles children can experience when they're giving it their best to learn and comprehend. These practices leave no room for change, growth, or even joy and wonder. Labels like these can devastate self-esteem and permanently damage potential before a child develops the cognizance to choose from their own consciousness or free will.

It doesn't help that many of our education systems have been squelched by dogmatic rules. We pass laws that place limits on human capacity. We base our knowledge on racist ideologies, religious and race superiority theories, economic status determinants, scientific biases, cultural elitism, environmental cruelty, and more. To quote the great Stephen Covey "You're on the wrong wall!!"

Many of our world's social structures, and systems, are skewed to failure because they are based on false premises. Those same structures force entire nations to suffer in abject poverty, disease, and disaster. While we stand idly by and look, armies form to protect that status quo. These false economies continue unchecked, at painful, exorbitant, and unrelenting human and environmental cost.

Meanwhile, many of our children languish in hostile environments they feel even more powerless than we do to inhabit, let alone change. They watch the adults in their lives and behave as they see us, no longer hearing, or heeding, the language of the heart.

They watch us choosing to escape reality in often unhealthy ways: abdicating our rights; refusing our responsibilities; denying our joy. Choosing to follow fear instead of love as the guiding force for everything. What's worse is we often model these behaviors, these choices, unconsciously, with the energy of negative, untrue judgments. In effect, we provide conflicting information to the young minds in our charge. Instead of blossoming a legacy of love with them, it's almost as though we perpetrate a family curse, creating enormous gaps of much needed knowledge, perspicacity, alacrity, wisdom, and always, always, more love.

These dichotomies of inhuman self-interest are what this book intends to guide us to stop creating unconsciously and start transforming consciously. We begin by healing our relationship with self-love.

In the vastness of the human experience, we sometimes overlook the relationships most precious to our hearts. That of our sacred privilege and responsibility to nurture all children. Exactly as they present themselves and with unconditional love.

Conscious Brain Training from your heart is a key to cultivating happiness and living up to that honorable task. Happiness fosters joy because we choose to show our strength through humility and self-mastery. We honor our imagination through creative collaboration.

We model how to keep hearts and minds open while learning perplexing concepts or traversing challenges. When we refocus our lens of vision to include all children, they know the truth of their worth and they can relax, too. Learning by heart becomes a cinch, together.

The children of our world need us present, awake, and listening with them. For they are uniquely equipped to tap into the vast fields of infinite solutions that love eternally gives us to choose from. We need to let them lead the way, be their willing students, and to let a growth mindset rooted in unconditional love be the guiding light for all our creations with and for our youth. Until they can hold the reins firmly on their own and we reach that pinnacle of parenthood.

It's time to teach them how to be a whole human and make conscious choices for the greater good through loving kindness. It's time to focus on what's good, right, and joyous, and to make more love. It's time to communicate with compassion and empathy. We must learn to learn again, remembering to watch when we are side-tracked from being our best, so we can pay attention to all the ways our children may get side-tracked from being at their best. We must support them as they ask questions, seeking the deepest truth for ourselves at the same time. Recognizing that learning and mastery are recursive. For life experiences can be integrated without trauma as our teacher. As we encourage ourselves to mature consciously, we activate that capacity for our children. It's time to create a world where the sun shines for one and all.

This book asks parents and teachers to reimagine how to teach and learn with their children. Instead of for them (and sometimes against everyone's best interests.)

It provides easy to follow steps for how to neutralize negative programs with compassion, joy, and love.

In the words of The Mind Aware creator, Dana Wilde, *"But the best benefit of training my brain is that I know how to stay emotionally aligned. I know how to be authentically, deeply happy. Happiness is something that all of us have at our fingertips. We generate happiness by the thoughts we think, and each of us can become a focused, proactive thinker."*

This book provides a plethora of practices, techniques, and evidence of how to train your own brain for health, happiness, success, and creativity. The authors have also provided a myriad of styles to play with and model in your relationships, in your parenting, in your teaching, and businesses.

The authors of this book are an eclectic group - some with degrees in medicine, education, public policy and more. Others with natural degrees, forged by lifetimes of communing with nature, parenting children, and lovingly crafting a life of joy through honest appreciation, trials, and sometimes tribulations. We are each passionate about families and children.

We want every child in the world to have their best chances at experiencing the school of life in joy, wonder, and being connected to others. We need the foundational energy of our family units intact for the future generations our children will guide.

The one thing we have in common is our desire to improve all our relationships and live happier, healthier, more joyful lives. We all decided to stop living same-old-same-old and step into new ways of thinking. We determined to retrain our minds and live fully. Vibrantly alive, right here, right now. No longer tempting fate but resourcing every ounce of goodness a healthy, conscious focus illuminates. (Biskind, 2018)

What many of us discovered, as you will from the heartfelt and very lived tales in this manuscript, is that we've had the power all along. We just didn't have the knowledge, at first, how paradigm shifts in thought could be possible. Or, what those same subtle changes in perception would do to improve the quality of our lives and the lives of those we love.

We decided that the universe of our minds is a friendly place. We committed to using our innate operating system of thought/feeling/focus as a self-governable, conscious technology. We made our own scientific discoveries and focused our natural resources to create tools and models for understanding that "universe of self" through loving, empowering, ennobling, conscious creation (Wallace, 2021). Power and safety come through understanding our inner workings and our deepest motives. That power, safety, and understanding are basic human rights.

Choosing to examine unconscious patterns of behaviors, beliefs, and attitudes is a first step into recovering your value, cultivating fields of unlimited possibilities, and collaborating with your true creative genius. For every human being intrinsically has the capacity to choose. The human brain is part of a whole system of life. It can and does, change, grow, evolve, adapt, learn, apply, and create anew. The human brain does not start dying at birth, as people once believed, if we'll allow it.

Retraining your brain uncovers some great key insights as to how to unlock our whole mind/body system's true power and potential. This is true for anyone, in any circumstance, at every age and stage of development. You don't need money, additional technology, or medical intervention.

Human beings of every age, stage, and status, have the power to change and transform their lives, even their very DNA! It is entirely possible, if you are willing to do the inner work and retrain your brain, lovingly. When you decide to cultivate sustainable states of mindful awareness, openness, self-love, and integrity, your brain and your life can be transformed.

It is akin to a beginner's mindset a.k.a. a growth mindset. That place or state of being where you approach life with gratitude, wonder, curiosity, and adventure. The results are a loving, sage, and open mind that most adults used to know well, the child's domain of infinite possibility, creativity, and joy. A disciplined mind is also flexible, honoring multiple points of view with respect. This is the kind of mind you want to model for your children. It is fresh, aware, and flexible. It is tapped in, turned on, and tuned up for success.

As you do, you will discover that what you may have known, experienced, or witnessed from your past stories, even historically or genetically, has no power to limit what you can create in the future. Brain training supports you to invite everyone in your circle of influence to participate wholeheartedly in their learning, especially your children. You and your child will learn how to make conscious choices, instead of just letting things happen.

Everything is energy. Energy requires direction. You always get to make a choice! You just may not know yet how you can change your mind and hone your focus from your whole heart through love. As you read this book and engage the practices, test, and try on some new approaches to your thinking, you will!

What we have discovered as a group, focusing on this singular intention to change our personal lives for the better, is how to allow the energy of thought to flow, toward and with, what we are consciously choosing. Learning how to hold the focus of love and joy on what we really, really want without attachment to outcome. Why? Because attaching an outcome or expectation changes the direction of the energy to one stuck in past beliefs not new creation.

We have discovered that deciding to change our habitual, unconscious thinking gives us the confidence to know and be able to quickly redirect any thought before it manifests into more of what we don't want.

We have also discovered how to teach conscious energy direction to our youth, instead of trying to "control" what has often been perceived as their "out of control" energy. We know that with more conscious thinking and a calm, quiet mind, we can redirect our reactions into positive responses. They can learn this, too!!! They are learning it from us anyway, even while still a baby in the womb. Why not make it explicit!?

You are always creating something. That something becomes manifested through the direction of your own energy. When your mind is secretly putting yourself down, talking trash, or cowering in fear because of unexamined beliefs, you are directing your energy toward disaster. You are polluting your own field and stifling your true creativity and potential.

Finding the energy to create solutions becomes even more elusive while your focus remains on the perceived problem and how "bad" you are at x, y, or z. You may even blame others for their bad behaviors which further justifies your crappy feelings. When you dig in your heels – "I'm right!" – this creates even more problems.

Training your brain can truly help you recognize the signs and muscle memory triggers before one of your autopilots, knee-jerk, nuclear reactionary outbursts rip another tear in the generation gap. Or hole in the ozone. Or overdraft withdrawal from your emotional bank accounts.

As just one family raises its consciousness, though, huge positive shifts can occur. As they recognize how to learn together by shifting from negative behavioral and autopilot thinking patterns into harmonious conscious choice, massive cultural shifts can happen. These imbalanced social systems are correctable in peaceful, creative, collaborative ways. One conscious, retrained, focused mind at a time.

Can you imagine a world where mutual respect and self-loving behaviors are the dominant rule of law? Wouldn't it be lovely to get to know our silent souls in harmony with our children? Would you kindly contemplate such a delicious state of living? Wouldn't conscious creation inspire more creativity and kinder community in joyful action?

There is so much more to know about Nature, the Cosmos, even our own human history, cultures, and peoples, than we've ever allowed ourselves to even consider.

Retraining our brains to guide ourselves to grow in more conscious awareness is a gift of love to ourselves and for our children's future. As George Benson (1977) so beautifully sang *"I believe the children are our future, teach them well and let them lead the way. Show them all the beauty they possess inside. Give them a sense of pride. Make it easier…"*

If you don't care, read no further. Medicare for All activist Ady Barkan states *"Hope is not a lottery ticket that we cling to. It's a hammer that we use in an emergency to break the glass, sound the alarm, and spring into action. Hope is action in the face of despair. Hope is born out of our insistence that a better world is possible and formed by our coming together in collective action to realize this better world of our imagination."* (2021, Democracy Now)

If you do care, are you ready to leap into a creative life that is willing to follow your heart? Are you inspired by your child every day? Are you sometimes saddened or feel defeated as a parent, a caregiver, a teacher, a human being? Fret no more.

We tell our simple stories here so you can begin your journey of living your own life as a brain trainer, a conscious creator, in the kind of world you choose for your children's future, freely. You get to live with an open heart that chooses love to guide your thinking, doing, and being, without worry. You get to step joyously into the unknown with enthusiastic appreciation for yourself and those you love. You get to wonder, learn, and be delighted along with your children, your students, and your relations in a more positive, productive fashion.

As authors and coaches, we are parents, teachers, leaders who choose to hold our focus on the goodness of life, and that the universe of our children's future is benevolent, beautiful, and bright. As Albert Einstein wrote to his colleague in 1942, there are only two choices: Love or Fear. And Love (or God) doesn't gamble with our lives, leave our future to chance, or abandon its children.

We shouldn't either. We choose to know ourselves, again or for the first time, as free to create consciously from all thought and all possibility. We get to reimagine, renew, resolve, and dissolve the patterns of pain and the addictions to suffering that have plagued our species and the Earth for far too long.

Together, we get to resurrect a world in peace, harmony, laughter, love, integrity, justice, and truthfulness, with balanced emotions, vibrant expressions, diverse solutions, health, wellness, economic equanimity, creativity, artistry, and true dignity for all life, everywhere.

Restoring a world where the complexities and conundrums that daily living often poses become clean fuel for conscious, collaborative change and wondrous discovery. Returning the mundane into the magnificent. Moving from perspectives born of devastating grief to gifts of love filled with generosity and gratitude.

For those who consistently retrain their brains to approach challenges from a state of neutrality of mind, and honest self-awareness, they get to create deep learning and intimate, loving relationships that flourish over time and across generations.

We see and respect all our children as the sovereign, free, already whole, and complete beings they truly are. We learn together with a beginner's mindset and set ourselves on the path of health, wellness, peace, and prosperity. We love and choose conscious communication. We consistently tackle the tough inner job as silent, private, personal work with bravery of heart.

In so doing, we all emerge victorious, homo evolutis on the wheel of co-creation (Marx Hubbard,1998/ Goodbaudy, 2012), joyful in our words and deeds. We become a mind/body/soul system on fire for Life and for Love.

Thank you for being here and testing how conscious creation works for yourself and your families, friends, colleagues, communities, governments, and more. You'll be glad you did!

Don't wait. Keep reading. This book is an easy read. Our goal is to have you rejoicing when you catch yourself in a negative thought or an entrenched pattern of unhappy outcomes because it means you are now raising your awareness!

We encourage you to remain determined to stay the course with the diligence and repetition of practice that mastering new skills requires. We hope you experience delight when you pause a vocal reaction that may be hurtful before it comes out of your mouth. May you be uplifted when you speak truth from your heart. And may you and all your family know ecstasy when you know your children "get" you, love you, and love themselves more just by being in your presence. And you them.

What a gift! You'll see.
Read on, today! You've got this!

CHAPTER 1

Train Your Brain for Parents

by Deborah C. Owen

Leaving squiggly, uneven tracks in the mud that was caked on his cheeks, tears streamed down Danny's face. His soccer team of 12-year-old boys had been playing in the rain - as they had nearly every week for most of the spring - and in his limited time on the field, he'd let the ball get past him... again... and his team had lost the game as a result. No matter how much his parents encouraged him and congratulated him for trying hard, none of it seemed to make a difference. He was miserable and despondent.

If you're a parent, you know at this point children tend to do one of two things. Either they totally clam up and refuse to engage with anyone else. Or they get extremely angry and lash out at everyone. And you can't predict which response you'll get because it could be one thing one day, and the opposite reaction the next!

As a parent, I'm sure you often struggle with how to help your children manage their emotions, especially in stressful situations like this. Perhaps you even struggle with managing your own emotions, since kids always seem to find the exact buttons to push that will drive you nuts.

And I'm sure you also know some people who seem to be followed around by a little black cloud; anything that can go wrong, does go wrong. I know a couple of people like that too!

What most people don't know is that life doesn't have to be like that. It doesn't have to be a daily dash for survival, madly careening from one activity to another - both kids' activities and adults' activities - with no real sense of purpose or joy.

In fact, most people you meet on the street - and maybe even in your neighborhood or at your office - have no idea that they get to choose how the day is going to go from the very moment their eyes open and their feet hit the floor.

What difference do you think it would make in your family if you were able to teach your children how they can choose their every reaction to the circumstances of life? How empowering for them to consciously know that they don't have to feel like "everyone's out to get me" (because most of them do feel that way!)?

What difference do you think it would it make in your own life if you had the ability to choose how you react to all the events of this crazy world in which you find yourself swirling?

Let's face it, the life of a parent today is busy. Our kids are busy... and we're busy too. Kids have more opportunities, expectations, challenges, and choices than ever before. And in fact, so do we, as parents. With all those extras comes more stress, and as you can see by Danny's reaction above, more opportunities for disappointment and frustration.

OK, now that I've pointed out the sadly obvious, I'd like to tell you that there is a way out of the madness. It's even, a little... subversive!

"The Secret" to Getting Kids' Attention

For twelve years, I worked as a public-school library teacher, most of that time teaching teenagers how to do research. (And you think your job is hard?) My husband of over 30 years and I have also raised three children of our own - complete with all the usual ups and downs, as well as some unusual challenges - and I must say, I wish I'd had the full benefit of what I'm about to share with you when I was actively raising

and teaching kids. I was only just beginning to discover the amazing power of the brain toward the end
of my child-raising and teaching years.

It started when I decided that to be the best teacher I
could possibly be, I needed to understand a bit of basic
brain science and how people learn. So, I went on a quest.

I won't bore you with all the ins and outs of where I
looked and what I read. Let's just say that from what I
discovered I became convinced that I'd been missing
out on something critical my entire life. I wondered
"Why no one was teaching this information??" Not
even to teachers!

As soon as I began implementing what I was
learning about the brain in my own life, I became a
more peaceful, joyful, focused person. I knew I had to
introduce these concepts to the teenagers in my life,
and as I began to apply them, it did make a difference,
especially at home.

At the time, our son, Christian, the youngest of our
three children, was in high school, while both his older
sister and brother were in college. Christian confided
in me at one point, "Brittany told me recently, 'I don't
know what's up with Mom, but I tell her stuff I didn't
used to tell her!'" That comment not only made my
day, but it also made my year!

Do you want to know the "secret" to getting your
kids' attention like that?

Well, in addition to reading a stack of positive
parenting books, I'd also begun implementing brain

training - for that's what it was - in all my interactions. Clearly, it was noticeable, even to my jaded teenage children. I had discovered the #1 key to changing how you feel - which changes how you react... which, in turn, changes the results you get in life.

That #1 key is this: You can always direct your thoughts and focus your energetic patterns.

This was a totally radical idea for me. I had always just tried to cope with whatever thoughts came my way. It never occurred to me that if I don't like my thoughts, I can change them. By changing them, I can honestly say I changed my life.

You see, your thoughts are the fuel in the engine that drives the rest of your life. Everything in your life. Nothing happens if you don't think it first and then associate a feeling to the thought. That negative or positive feeling associated with the thought is the true determiner of outcomes.

For example, if the first thing you think about when you wake up is how busy your day is going to be, well, you don't have much of a chance to have a less busy day, do you?

If you go into an exam thinking "I'm going to bomb", it's nigh impossible to be at your very best to do well.

If you approach a meeting with a potential client thinking you wish you'd had more time to be prepared, you'll likely feel unprepared the entire meeting.

And, if you expect your child to give you a hard time, you'll likely start out the interaction in either defensive or offensive mode, neither of which bodes well for a good interaction.

The underlying problem in all these scenarios is the thought process immediately before they begin.

"The problem is not the problem. The problem is talking about the problem, thinking about the problem. FOCUSING on the problem and recreating the negative beliefs and feelings associated with the problem." (Wilde, 2013)

Consider the potential differences if you think instead, "I'm going to have a great day today!" or "I've done all the studying I can and I am going to do my very best", or "I am confident we can solve this prospect's core problem", or "I'm going to let Danny know how much I love him this morning."

In the same way I changed my thinking patterns - which meant I FELT differently about myself, which is also important - you, too, can change your thoughts.

In short, if you don't like the results you're getting, you get to choose which thoughts you have.

Let's break it down a bit more, with some...

Basic Brain Science

Your conscious mind, which processes information at about 40 bits per second, is the part that allows you to learn, remember, plan, set goals, create, imagine, make decisions, complete tasks, and generally think about things. It's the part of your brain that gives you an identity; it seems that what you think about is "you."

The truth is, it's really your unconscious mind (also known, inaccurately, as the subconscious mind), that is most responsible for your autonomous body and brain functions at any given moment. The unconscious mind is as much as 95% of your brain activity right now, while only about 5% is aware of your surroundings, your senses, or the words on this page.

Your unconscious mind processes around 40 million bits per second, far more than your conscious mind is capable of processing. One of its biggest jobs is to run all your body systems in the background - such as your digestion, cell growth, blood flow, bodily reactions, and functions, etc. - so you don't have to think about them. Once you learn how to do common tasks - such as tying your shoes, brushing your teeth, and even driving your car - it helps you do them automatically, without having to waste precious brain energy thinking about them. Additionally, our unconscious mind is the repository for memories, beliefs, value systems, and more.

Ironically, however, your unconscious mind is also ultimately in charge of most of your conscious thought processes. It takes the conscious thoughts you have - "I have to study for that exam, or I'll fail"; "My son is having a terrible day today" - and stores them in the unconscious "well" of beliefs. This well is deep, and once ensconced down there, it's challenging to get that thought out of the well.

Here's An Example of What Happens

Eight-year-old Danny is excited to play soccer. All his friends are signing up, so he begs his parents to let him sign up also. At the first practice, he trips over his shoelace and lands flat on his face. A bunch of the kids laugh ("Better him than me", they think), and he's ashamed of himself for being an apparent klutz. As a result, he stops trying very hard that day, so he doesn't draw attention to himself anymore.

At the succeeding practices, he continues to hide behind the other players, afraid of making a mistake. By the end of the season, he's not kept up with the more aggressive players on his team and falls behind in his skillset. "I'm not a good soccer player" he tells himself. And the other players confirm that message by what they say and how they act toward him.

Jump ahead a few years. Danny is 12 now, still hanging out with his friends on the soccer field, even though the coach doesn't put him in to play very often. Is it any wonder that when he does get on the field the negative recording in the back of his mind is, "I'm a bad soccer player! I keep missing shots and blocks and I hope it doesn't lead to the other team winning!"

Danny grows up a bit and goes to college. There's a pick-up soccer league on his campus. When they're looking for players, do you think Danny jumps in? It's highly unlikely, because he has a conscious recording in his brain saying, "I was always a terrible soccer player. I never could get my foot on the ball, and I always gave away the win to the other team. I'd better not join and let down this new team too. What would the girls think of me?"

You get the picture. It's usually ONE bad experience, ONE negative comment from someone, ONE self-defeating thought that doesn't get switched around, and it repeats and repeats and repeats... Potentially, for the rest of your life.

Think about your own thoughts for just a moment. Before you picked up this book and started reading, how many positive vs. negative thoughts did you have? How many times do you berate yourself in your head and call yourself names? (i.e., "I can't believe I did that! I'm such an idiot!")

The key thing is, when you don't stop yourself from thinking something that may be untrue by saying - "That's crazy! I'm not really like that!" - it's as if you agree with the negative, untrue thought. By helping to solidify that thought, especially if you think it multiple times and continue agreeing with it, it becomes part of your identity. The negative belief is now how you define yourself. It also becomes how others define you because it becomes the energy we project.

Thinking positive thoughts vs. negative thoughts makes a really big difference. Shockingly, even if you think of yourself as a generally positive person, most of your thoughts are negative. It's a protection mechanism left over from cave person days when humans were scanning their environment for danger.

To make matters even worse, your conscious mind repeats almost all the same thoughts - positive or negative - all day, every day, day after day, year after year.

A 2005 National Science Foundation article concluded the average person has anywhere from 12,000 to 60,000 thoughts per day (I'm not quite sure how they measure this, but when I think about my own thoughts, I believe it!). This study found that 80% of this "mental chatter" is negative and about 95% of your thoughts are the identical, repetitive thoughts you had the day before, the day before that, and twenty years ago! Talk about getting into a rut!

It is just like a path through tall grass. The more often you walk in the exact same steps as the day before, the more clearly you see the path. When you travel on it repeatedly, the path becomes easier and faster, until it's practically a superhighway from one end to the other, with nothing stopping you!

The more you practice these thoughts, the more ingrained they become until they become deep-seated beliefs, stuck in that well, just like Danny's beliefs about being a bad soccer player.

So how do you STOP this craziness, which is making you unhappy?

To continue the metaphor, you must clear a new pathway through that tall grass. It won't be easy at first; it takes time to cut down the weeds in front of you, and that other pathway right nearby is so much easier to navigate… But you get to choose your destination. The results you don't like, or the results you want. The thought pathway for each is different because they end in different places.

That now brings up the question, what results DO you want to see in your life? How do you begin to bring those desired, advantageous results into existence instead?

The Reticular Activating System (RAS)

Because the human brain is quite literally inundated with millions of bits of information every moment of the day, you would be completely overwhelmed and unable to function if there weren't a filter. This filter is called the reticular activating system or RAS. It's a network of neurons in your brain stem connecting your spinal cord, cerebrum, and cerebellum. The primary job of the RAS is to filter OUT all the extraneous information you don't need to pay attention to, and filter IN what you think is important.

What you think about most often, MUST be most important… right? Well, as we've seen already, that's not necessarily so!

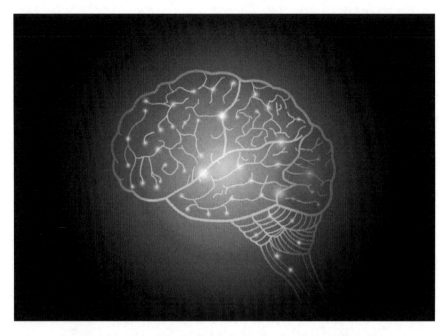

Figure 3: *The Human Brain Adobe Stock License to Deborah C Owen*

Whatever you're thinking about, combined with how you feel about it, creates an internal picture of your world. And the RAS, little matchmaker that it is, is intent on matching up your internal picture with your external picture - what you're experiencing, feeling, and focused upon - to create cognitive congruence (and avoid cognitive dissonance!). Those two pictures - internal and external - MUST match, or you feel "uncomfortable" or "unsettled".

In fact, that internal picture, once created, is very "sticky". If that thought path is traveled often enough, and you agree with the thought enough, and you even experience strong emotions because of that thought, it transforms into a deep-seated belief that gets really stuck in that "well" in your brain. Even if you encounter evidence to the contrary, you are unable to recognize the truth of that evidence if it doesn't match your internal belief.

For instance, even though Danny had trouble with soccer early on, he might likely try his hand at another sport. If he excels at baseball and basketball, it's possible he could still say to himself, "I'm a terrible soccer player. There's no way I'd ever be any good at it." Maybe this is true… but if he's a natural athlete in other sports, he's probably blind to the idea that he could get better in soccer… if he wanted to.

Add to this mix the fact that emotionally charged experiences are more easily remembered - and bond like glue, to make those thoughts and beliefs sticky, stuck and looping like a robot on auto-repeat. You can see why the humiliation Danny felt when he was 8 years old really stayed with him and helped form this sticky belief of unworthiness. So sad, really.

When it comes to the RAS, the most important thing to know is this: Your inside world - your thoughts and beliefs - and your outside world - what you experience - MUST match, and your RAS will do everything it can to make whatever you believe show up over and over in your actual environment.

As you might imagine, this unconscious need for congruence even effects how you act. No matter what situation you're in, your brain knows exactly what to do because, "That's the type of person I am (or am not)." Everything you place after those words "I am..." creates our RAS's definition of who you are. You can continue with devastating, unhappy results, or consciously create a fulfilling life complete with legacies of lasting peace.

In other words, because of the need to make an internal/external match, your unconscious mind, through your RAS, is what defines yourself self-identity: "I'm an introvert"; "I'm not very smart"; "I'm the class clown"; "I hate math because I'm not very good at it". On and on the loop goes. Unless, and until, you consciously start to formulate different thoughts and feelings. Retraining your brain and the ways you "talk to yourself" is how you transform your life. It's also how you teach your children to consciously do the same.

Fine... Now What?

You can easily find all the information I've just shared with you up to this point by poking around on the internet, and by picking up a couple of books about psychology and the brain. But knowing all this information isn't always going to get you where you want to go. It's mostly theory without a way to turn things around.

What made the difference for me, and how you, too, can apply these new understandings in your life is a program I discovered called Train Your Brain, by entrepreneur and amateur brain science aficionado, Dana Wilde (2013).

You may be wondering why a teacher like me would trust a brain training program from an entrepreneur, instead of from a scientist. That's a fair question.

The first answer is, "it works" for me. Period. Take that for what it's worth.

The second answer is because Dana Wilde is like you and me in many respects. She worked in the corporate world for a while and wasn't sure what she wanted to "do" with her life. It was during that time she "stumbled" onto the science of brain training. After discovering that the way you THINK creates your outcomes, she decided to apply what she had learned in her own life.

Taking brain training on the road, Dana traveled the world, lived overseas for the better part of a decade, became a published author at 23, worked in the film industry and won two Telly Awards, and then started her own business, which grew to annual sales of a million dollars in record time. No one else in that company has ever come close. How did she accomplish so much, so successfully? After she learned about brain training, Dana realized, "I knew I could do anything I wanted to do with my life, and I would always land on my feet."

Oh, wait. Do you mean you haven't made a million dollars in record time for your company yet?

Well, as I said, that's the second reason I paid attention to Dana's formula. She's an "everywoman" kind of person who completely changed her life - that relatively quick million dollars thing - when she developed this surprisingly simple brain training formula.

It wasn't long before she began teaching the program on its own, first to her own team members for her business, and then to thousands of other people, who discovered they could apply it to many aspects of life, not just to building a business from scratch. That is how this book was born.

A group of us in Dana's Train Your Brain program discovered that the very same system you can use to grow a business can also be used to develop an amazing relationship with your kids (and your spouse!).

In fact, when you teach this program to your kids, you can, quite literally, set them on a completely different path - one probably more successful and happy - than if they didn't know and practice these skills.

It is truly a brain training program. Here's the formula (and then I'll explain it):

1. Be aware of your thoughts
2. Decide - do you want your RAS to keep matching this up?
3. Talk about the current situation in a way that feels good
4. Cultivate positive emotions

That's the core of the program, just four steps.

Step 1 is easy to understand now that you know how your unconscious mind governs most of your thinking. Your mind goes on autopilot and repeats the same negative thoughts day after day. By becoming aware of your thoughts, you simply can and will catch yourself thinking a negative thought!

Step 2 is when you ask yourself, "Do I want my reticular activating system to keep matching up that thought? How do I feel after I have that thought? If I feel bad, I should probably change it!"

Step 3 is how to change up your language, which we'll get to in just a moment.

Step 4 acknowledges that you don't want to feel bad; you want to feel good. You can achieve this goal by changing your thoughts, and, over time, even changing what you believe, especially about yourself.

OK, we're still a little short on steps 3 and 4. This is the stuff you can't just find in other books and resources. The place to find them is in *Train Your Brain* (the book and/or the online program).

Cycle of Perpetual Sameness

When you just "know" something about yourself, it means you agree with that thought and belief over and over. It becomes entrenched in that well in your unconscious mind, and it is very difficult to get it out.

This belief can be good or bad. It can be, "I am a good student" or "I am not a good student". You can imagine the many thoughts your child would need to have to develop either one of these identities/beliefs!

The more often you repeat a thought, the more stuck that belief gets, and the more you act it out automatically, without even thinking about it, especially if there is some level of emotion wrapped up in that belief. Remember, your unconscious mind needs to match up your internal beliefs with your external world.

When you don't like your results, you berate yourself - that's your reaction - and start calling yourself names ("What's my problem?"; "Dang it, I procrastinated again"; "Why can't I ever hand things in on time?").

Unfortunately, in this case (fortunately, in other cases), your unconscious mind can't tell the difference between what's real and what's imagined, so the more you repeat a thought/belief, the stickier it becomes. The more you attach emotion to the thought, the more your RAS looks for ways to match up your internal and external worlds.

As you can see in the diagram below, your unconscious mind matches up your beliefs with your outside world reality, thereby creating your behavior, which creates the results in your life.

Voila, the Cycle of Perpetual Sameness!

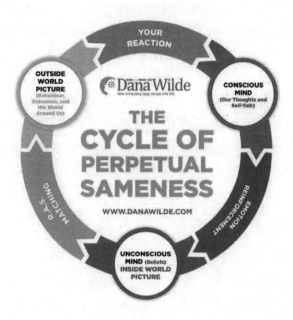

Figure 4: *Graphic courtesy of Dana Wilde (2013, p. 65)*

OK, now that you see the patterns, you can see why it's a much better idea to create beliefs that make you happy! I know I'd much rather get happy thoughts and beliefs into the Cycle than negative ones.

Well, how do I do that? How do I stop the negative cycle and transform it into a positive cycle?

While your unconscious mind runs your life, you can interrupt those automatic negative thoughts consciously, by reprogramming your thought patterns with new messages.

Steps 1 and 2, above, are to become aware of your thoughts and then decide to change them. So far so good.

Step 3 is the key to the pattern interrupt. Catch yourself saying something negative and then state something positive instead. This is called a mantra, and it does two important things:

1. It keeps your mind occupied with positive thoughts (you can't think of two things at once!)
2. It reprograms your unconscious mind which, with repetition, creates a new pathway in your brain.

THE WAY you say it is important. This is when it is fortunate that your unconscious mind can't tell the difference between real and imagined! Here are the four guidelines for perfect language mantras:

1. State it in the positive
2. State it as if it has already happened or been resolved
3. State something that is believable
4. Go for positive emotional impact, nothing wishy-washy.

That last guideline is essential. If your mantra doesn't elicit a powerful positive emotion - joy, happiness, excitement, etc. - it won't be effective. Let's look at some examples.

"Math is fun and easy."

"I am a very good student in social studies."

"I am becoming more and more patient with my kids every day."

"Every day I'm getting clearer and clearer about where I want to go to college."

"Being present with the family at dinner is one of the best times of my day."

"I'm getting better and better at soccer every day."

"I have enough energy for my homework because I eat a good dinner first."

I don't have time or space here to go into all the nuances of perfect language mantras. But I think you get the idea that it must have a continuous, ongoing action; you don't want to use words like "might" or "want to"; it should be a bit on the general side; and to make it believable to your unconscious, you can use softening phrases like, "better and better" or "more and more". (To get more details on perfect language mantras, I recommend reading Train Your Brain by Dana Wilde or joining her mailing list to receive a weekly positivity rant.)

Once you create this mantra, for as long as it makes you feel good, and keeps you excited to get going, repeat it as a neutralizer to the negative thought/feeling patterns you are transforming. Repeat it often and with conviction. After all, you're trying to create a new pathway to travel in your brain!

Let me be clear: **The whole point of brain training is to feel good.** Biologically, when you feel good, the creative pathways in your brain are open and you literally have access to better ideas. You have more energy. You like people better and feel like engaging. And you are much more likely to match up the fun and success you think about, with fun and success in your external world. Dana has earned millions of dollars - and has tens of thousands of proteges - to prove that changing your thoughts and feeling good works.

Now What?

I told you this "secret" would be a bit "subversive", and I think it is! You're breaking and transforming the Cycle of Perpetual Sameness (Wilde, 2013) by using the natural powers of your unconscious mind. Because our body/mind is incapable of telling real from imaginary, your new conscious positive mantra is repeating now what you really want to experience in your life. It's as if you already have accomplished or mastered it. This transformative brain training process helps you consciously create new pathways of juicy stickiness now so that your little matchmaker, the RAS*, will continue constantly matching up what you think about most often. Now, you and your RAS create what you truly, and consciously, choose to manifest in the real world.

In summary:

- Notice your thoughts
- Decide whether you want your RAS to filter in what your thoughts are generating and match up your experiences, your relationships, and your outcomes with those thoughts
- Create a mantra that will give you the results you truly desire and that make you excited
- Repeat that mantra as many times every day as you can remember

When it comes to your kids, they probably won't want to hear all these steps and all the details about how to be happier and more joyful in life. You're going to have to model this for them. And that's what the next chapters are all about.

They are written by people in the *Train Your Brain* program who have some expertise in parenting, raising kids, and being a parent.

If you have kids, or you work with kids, or you have grandkids, neighbors, or nieces and nephews, I believe there is no greater gift in life than the power to change their thoughts from negative to positive. It will dramatically alter the course of their lives.

Think about that. I say it in all seriousness.

As I've been considering life missions lately, I've been starting to ask people what they are passionate about. When people ask me what I am passionate about, I reply that it's simple. I am passionate about helping kids and families find more love and joy in their lives.

I am constantly on the lookout - and so is my RAS! - for new ways to achieve this goal. Sharing this book with you is one of the best ways I know how to do that.

Please read the following chapters that apply to you, and start to implement them in your life, and in the lives of your children. Refer to this chapter often when you need a refresher on how your brain works.

CHAPTER TWO

Respecting Your Child's Hunger and Fullness Cues

by Angela Humburg MS, RDN, LD

My second daughter was born a full-term healthy baby with a slightly yellow tint to her skin. Apparently, that means there's a problem in the liver. Because of this, the doctor ordered a special "bilirubin-light" and regular blood work to ensure the bilirubin numbers were going down.

I dutifully followed her doctor's orders while I continued to breastfeed. After several blood draws with no significant change in her numbers, the doctor recommended I add infant formula. (Evidently, formula helps a baby poop more, which removes excess bilirubin.) Alas, however, my daughter didn't dutifully follow the doctor's orders like I did! She didn't like the taste of formula or having a bottle shoved in her mouth when she wasn't hungry. She cried and spit and ultimately refused to drink the bottle. As a result, I got stressed. I called my sister who is a pediatric nurse. I lamented to my mom. I asked for my friends' advice. I searched the internet. Ugh. The more advice I got, the more stressed I became.

But here's what I later noticed: my daughter wasn't stressed. She didn't care what the numbers were. She didn't mind that her skin looked like she had rolled in dandelions. She wasn't going to drink the formula. Period. I learned a new version of the old saying, "I could lead my baby to the bottle, but I couldn't make her drink."

I often hear from parents who experience similar stresses, because of their children's anthropometric "numbers". As a society, we put a lot of emphasis on numbers such as height, weight, pants size, and shoe size. Maybe a parent is shown a height/weight graph and her child plots at a high percentile. Another parent may be concerned that her 3-month-old doesn't consume the "recommended" ounces/milliliters of formula.

What if you never knew where your baby plotted on the graph? What if you never measured your 13-year-old son and had no idea how tall he was? What if you breastfed and had no clue how many milliliters your infant consumes? What would happen to your son or daughter? Nothing. Because your child's amazing brain would maintain your child's height, weight, shoe, and pant size just as it should. Our brains are amazing at maintaining homeostasis! And, just like my daughter, your child wouldn't stress a bit. You wouldn't, either!

Unless a baby has a conflicting medical diagnosis, we ALL know that it's time to eat when we physically need fuel. Your brain is also wired to signal you to stop eating once you are full or satisfied. This is called Intuitive Eating and was first introduced by world-renowned registered dietitian nutritionists Evelyn Tribole and Elyse Resch (2020).

Infants may not be able to verbalize when they're satisfied, but they give us all kinds of evidence. As parents, we must increase our awareness. A baby may turn his head from the bottle or fall asleep at the breast. When the baby is being fed baby food, she may start throwing food or spitting it with great delight when she's full. It doesn't matter if she's throwing away "good money" or messing up your clean floor. She's full. Food has no value to her once she's full. At that point, it may become a form of entertainment. And it likely becomes a form of frustration for you, the parent. You may lament, "She ate two whole jars yesterday. What's wrong with her today? She hardly ate anything this morning. Is she sick?"

You may get nervous and don't want to see the "wrong" numbers, so you teach your children to ignore their brains' hunger or satiety signals. You may also ignore the signs they give you. You may try to train them to hit the "override button" on the part of their brain that controls hunger/satiety. And, after repeatedly overriding their brains, your children learn to ignore the fact that they are either not physically hungry or that they are uncomfortably full.

As parents, you may unknowingly bestow other "voices" of hunger on your children. You may teach them as infants to "finish this little bit" of formula because he/she is just 5% weight/height. They learn to eat past the point of satisfying their hunger. You may give them a bottle whenever they cry to keep them quiet. They learn to distract themselves with food. You may wake up in the middle of the night and give them a bottle when they are physiologically old enough to be sleeping through the night, and then they learn to equate food with comfort. You may tell your toddler to eat all their vegetables before they are allowed to eat dessert, and then they learn that food is a reward.

Don't fret if you've been in these situations. You and your child's unconscious minds can be reprogrammed with some simple strategies.

First, it is simply your job to offer a variety of healthy foods for your child in a positive environment. You are responsible for offering those healthy foods at set times throughout the day. (Often these are three meals and 2-3 snacks.) Second, it's your child's job to decide if she's going to eat or not and if she does eat, how much. Did you read that? It said "if". Your job is not to make your child eat! Your job is not to insist she eats "five more bites". You are not to tell her that she can only have dessert once she eats all her broccoli.

Your job is to help her recognize and respect her powerful brain signals that tell her when she's hungry. Your job is to respect those signals and offer her nourishing options. Your job is to be aware of the cues she gives when she's satisfied. That means that some days, when she's going through a growth spurt or when she's running all over the place, she eats like a professional football player. And that's ok! That also means there will be some meals and some whole days when she's not very hungry and she eats like a bird. That's ok as well!

Each of us has had a child who ate like the two mentioned above at one time or another. And that child went on to eat the next snack or meal just fine. As was mentioned in Deborah Owen's introduction to brain training, with awareness, a positive feeding environment and repetition, you and your child will learn to focus on the enjoyment of eating nourishing food without stressing. You will become an expert at recognizing the signals she gives when she is physically hungry and feel at ease when she stops eating because her brain signals satiety.

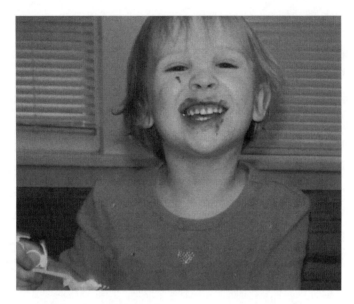

Figure 4: *Angela Humburg's Baby Girl*

CHAPTER THREE

Sticky Notes for Focus

by Patricia Dawn Clark

Have you ever wanted something so badly that you focused all your thoughts and attention on it? I used to do this a lot. I'd think about how I didn't have it, and then I'd wonder how I would ever get it. I would waste time and energy thinking about how I could achieve it faster, and then still wonder, "Why isn't this happening right now?!!?" Never content with what I had, I never felt good. I felt like there was always something else I wanted and didn't have. Like I was missing out on something.

For instance, there was the time I was working toward a specific goal with my business, earning a trip for two for a week to an all-inclusive resort. I desperately wanted to achieve this goal! My husband and I had never gone anywhere like that, and I thought it would be so much fun to take him.

I slowly recognized my general state of discontent. Not wanting to stay there, I discovered a brilliant and simple process that helped me keep the outcome I truly wanted to achieve in the forefront of my mind. That was "the experience of spending the week with him and earning the trip." I chose to focus on what I really wanted, instead of all the stress of how to make it happen.

I took about 10 sticky notes and wrote a sentence on each one, such as "Earning the trip is so easy," or "We enjoy our time together on an exotic island," ending with a "ta-da!" or "Hooray!" Then I posted them all over the house. They were on the coffee maker, the microwave, the bathroom mirrors, the front door, my steering wheel - anywhere I would see it consistently throughout my day. Whenever I saw the note, I would say the sentence out loud, and I would feel the feeling of excitement and energy that came with imagining the accomplishment of that goal. This went on for months as I went about my work and life. In the end, I did earn the trip, and my husband and I enjoyed the beautiful vacation I had seen in my mind's eye.

What I did not realize at the time was that my children were watching me. (They always are, aren't they?) I soon discovered other notes around the house of reminders they wanted to keep in their minds. I found notes of lists of what they wanted to do after school or a positive phrase they wanted to keep thinking. As a family, we would often make a bucket list for summer vacation or winter break, but this was the first time I saw them posting reminders for themselves as they went about their days.

We were able to talk about how the notes I had posted worked for me. I stopped focusing on what I didn't have, and focused, instead, on feeling good. They really liked how simple this was. Now, we make notes for anything they want more of in their life. Struggling with a specific assignment in school? Post "Every day, I am learning and growing," or "I learn exactly what I need at the right time." Maybe they are having trouble making new friends or feeling included in their current friend group. They can post "Good friends find me easily," or "I love making new friends." They especially enjoy adding a "magic word" at the end like I did with "ta-da!" or "hooray!"

It really does feel a bit like magic. When you focus on what you want and what you are expecting, rather than on what you don't yet have, you make your brain go to work for you. That RAS (Reticular Activating System; the information filter in your brain) is set into motion, and you begin to match up what you are thinking with what you see in the world.

As I have seen firsthand, this is such a powerful tool for your children to have as they grow up! I wish

I had known this when I was younger. No more time wasted on unhappy thoughts! The sticky notes don't do anything for you except interrupt your day and remind you to keep what you expect right there, top-of-mind. You don't have any energy left to worry or wonder. You can feel that powerful, positive energy that comes with achieving your visions.

Children are naturally powerful in their imaginations. You can help them keep that power as they grow with this simple action of sticky notes for focus. And who knows, you may find you are all accomplishing amazing things together as a family. Changing the world together!

CHAPTER FOUR

Who Knew?

by Deborah Helser

I grew up as the fourth child in a family of six children. I am one of the four girls in our family. I say this because it wasn't a lavish lifestyle that was afforded to my siblings and me, but I felt rich nonetheless, due in part to my mom's positive affirmations and mantras. My mom did not know that that is what she was doing, for it was back in the late fifties (for me). But she, and my dad for that matter, always chose the positive!

I can hear mom now, singing, *"You've got to Ac-Cent-Tchu-Ate, the positive and EEEE-LIM-IN-ATE the negative."* (Arlen & Mercer 1944) Whenever my siblings and I had issues, or we had problems with friends or classmates, we were always reminded about the Golden Rule: *"Do unto others as you would have them do unto you."* This may seem a bit "old school" but as a child, when you hear these words from your parents, and they model that behavior as well, it really sticks with you!

Figure 6: *Deborah's loving parents, Stanley E. & Helen (Kasprzyk) Muszynski on their wedding day*

Flash forwards some twenty years to when I have three children of my own. I knew I wanted to instill those same ideals. I asked myself the question, "Why did I respect and love my parents so much?" "How did they get me to not want to disappoint them?" I pinpointed a few things.

First, they always told me that no matter what I did in life, they would always love me. Children need to hear this; tell them how much they mean to you and that they are loved. It sounds simple, but don't let life's busyness cause you to forget to reassure them they are loved, every day!

Second, I learned from my mom's very simple, but never failing, "morning goodbye" ("Have a great day and God be with you!") that I could positively "brainwash" (AKA: Brain Train) my own children. Hearing those words every day as I headed out the door were so very comforting and memorable. I wanted to instill that kind of comfort and confidence in my children too.

Third, my parents believed in the saying, "United we stand; divided we fall!" and always supported each other. This sent a clear message to my siblings and me that it was pointless to try to play them off each other. Other sayings that impacted my young brain were, "Say what you mean and mean what you say!" and "Think before you speak!"

As a new mom, I read a lot of parenting magazines looking for great parenting tips. One of the terrific ideas I learned was to read to your children every night at bedtime, and then ask two specific questions: "What was the worst, bad, or most challenging part of your day?" and "What was the best, happiest, or most successful part of your day?" Then, really hear them from a neutral, loving state of active listening.

In addition to having great conversations when your kids are young and helping them process the ups and downs of life, the article stated that if you do this regularly with young children, by the time they get to be teenagers, they won't think it's weird if you pop in before bedtime to have a conversation. My children are now 28, 30, and 32, and when asked, they say they remember doing this, and always looked forward to that time of day.

Another great tip I learned was how to get your child to slow down and speak clearly to you. My first child was attending a Catholic preschool where she learned a prayer. When I couldn't understand what she was saying, I asked her to teach it to me. I explained she'd have to go a bit slower and say each word as mommy wrote them down. She was thrilled to be the "teacher" and was very patient with her "student"! Here is that prayer she taught me:

"Good morning, Jesus, Good Morning, Mary, I give to you this day, all my work and all my play. Keep me safe by night and day!"

Simple, yet aren't prayers somewhat mantra-like?

As our family grew to three children, we not only said this prayer every morning (even as we were running for the bus, lol) but I added to it once I started my job as a teacher's aide in the school my children attended. You see, I was then able to have them ride with me instead of on the bus every morning!

This is when the "Golden Rule" was added, as well as my "Honesty is the best policy" and "An honest person is brave" mantras. They were a captive audience as they rode to school every morning, so why not? Here is how our daily "Morning Prayer/ Mantra" went:

> All: "Good morning, Jesus, Good Morning, Mary, I give to you this day, all my work and all my play. Keep me safe by night and day!"
>
> Mom: "What's the best policy?"
>
> Kids: "Honesty!"
>
> Mom: "And an honest person is _____?"
>
> Kids: "Brave!"
>
> Mom: "That's right! Be brave today and always!"

Of course, we had conversations about these topics (being honest; how it is so important to always tell the truth; treat others how you'd want to be treated) before it boiled down to this repeated daily activity/mantra. They can repeat it back to me to this day! As my mom's simple "Morning Goodbye" had stuck with me, so has our "Morning Prayer" mantra stuck with my children. Oh, and if you are wondering if I also said my mother's words to my kids, ("Have a great day and God be with you") yes, I did that as well! Those were the last words they heard from me as we parted for the day.

My third point is best illustrated by our "Ride to the Fair," as I'll call it. The whole family was headed to the big County Fair. The children were all excited and acting out, as siblings sitting next to each other sometimes do. (Who am I kidding? More often than not!) My husband warned them if they didn't stop acting out, we were NOT GOING TO THE FAIR! And of course… they did it again.

I told my husband to turn the car around and head back home. He asked "Why?" I reminded him that we had to follow through on what he'd said: if they didn't stop, we weren't going to the Fair. They didn't stop, so we had to hold to our word. He certainly learned to "Think before he speaks" after that! Being consistent and doing what you say you're going to do is one of the most challenging parts of parenting, but one of the most important. Remember to, "Say what you mean and mean what you say." Keep this mantra in the forefront of your parenting repertoire and you'll have fewer battles; your children will learn early on that you mean business.

Here are a few more ideas that made a difference for our family:

- When planning a special trip, tell your children you are going on an "adventure". This way if you need to change plans due to unexpected circumstances, there won't be any disappointment because they will not know anything was changed.

- When a child has a strong grip on something you'd like them to let go of, it helps to empower them and give them choices that you are comfortable with. For instance, if you want the child to let go of a pencil, they have a death grip on, tell him/her they can either put it in your hand or place it on the table. I can almost guarantee that the child will choose the table EVERY TIME! Choices on your terms are always better than ultimatums.

Figure 6: *Here is Deborah with her siblings at her son Scott's wedding in 2015; picture credit to Kathy Rozewski-Trzecieski*

- Identify your child's feelings because that shows you care and have heard them. Trust me when I say a child will "get over it" sooner than later when you do. If they fall and hurt themselves instead of saying "That didn't hurt." say, "That must have hurt, how can I help you feel better?" Sympathize, then move on.

These tips will help you enjoy being with your children every day!

One final quote/mantra from my dad:

**"Nothing to it, but to do it,
set your mind to it!"**

CHAPTER FIVE

Tips to Master the "Magical Matchmaker"

by Kristin A. Carbone

How is it you can get yourself dressed in the morning, make breakfast for yourself and the kids AND help find the missing shoe? All the while your lungs breathe in and out. Oxygen flows to all your extremities. Plus, your digestive system works on digesting your breakfast too! It all works so smoothly because your brain is on "autopilot" all day long. Well, most of your brain that is! Another part of your brain on "autopilot "is the Reticular Activating System, or RAS.

I like to call it a "magical matchmaker".

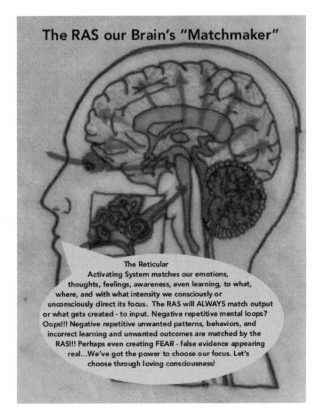

Figure 8: *The Magical Matchmaker (RAS) by LACR*

The RAS matches up whatever you're thinking about or talking about. Then, like magic more of what you're thinking or talking about starts to show up in the world around you.

You see, what we resist, persists. How we believe, we receive. We have the power to recognize subconscious, unconscious, or auto-pilot beliefs, programs, or ideas, and then, train our brains to model for our families how we truly are the captains of our ship, the masters of our destiny, and conscious creators.

**TIP #1:
You Need to Switch Off All "Autopilot" Thinking

Let me explain. If you were to say to someone, "Hey, check out that cool red car!" your RAS would go to work for you. Its response would be, "OK, you want to see more red cars… here you go!" You will notice red cars everywhere.

"How to Manifest Anything You Want in 72 Hours" is a brain training experiment you can try with your child. It will help you both understand how powerful the "magical matchmaker" is. You first decide on an object you want your RAS to focus on and bring into your awareness for the next 72 hours.

When I did this experiment for the first time, I chose a blue feather for the object I wanted to "see." I repeated the phrase, "I see blue feathers everywhere" several times a day for 72 hours. In less than three days, I saw blue feathers all over the place! Feathers on the ground, in pictures, and even on a t-shirt! It was fun and easy… and it worked!

For my daughter Makayla's experiment, she chose the Volkswagen Beetle "Punch Bug." Not a car you see out on the road often, but like magic she spotted several during her 72-hour experiment. She would get so excited whenever she spotted "her car." Of course, my arm was not so excited about all the punch bug punches, but that's a story for another time. My daughter had firsthand proof of how the "magical matchmaker" works. She learned the skill of creating through her own intentional thoughts. This gave her confidence to take back control. No more autopilot!

**TIP #2:
Use Mantras to Change Your Thinking

Mantras are another tool you can use to manifest something, to change a situation, or to change a belief. Mantras are phrases you repeat throughout the day. You are training your RAS to do its "magical matchmaking thing". To bring into your life what you think about most. A good mantra must be in the present tense ("I am..."). They should be thoughts with feel-good emotions, which lifts your spirit and helps boost your RAS because positive emotions are important when training your RAS!

When working with kids, allow them to use their imagination to create fun and playful mantras. You want to repeat your mantra many times throughout the day. You could have your child turn their mantra into a song, or have it rhyme – something easy for them to remember. It makes it easy to repeat and takes little effort. Repeating the mantra will send the mantra to the autopilot part of the brain – the RAS (reticular activating system).

Also try using Sticky notes as reminders. My daughter and I posted our mantras all over the house. We placed Sticky notes on her closet door, the bathroom mirror, the refrigerator, and on coat hooks. We even posted one in the car! Give your child the freedom to pick where they would like to post their mantra. Get creative and a little wild with this one!

It's helpful to point out to your child how their mantras are working. If your child has been saying a mantra about making a friend, point out the signs. For example, your child talks to a new kid on the playground. Someone from their class made a nice comment on their social media. How about when your child makes it to the bus stop on time with all their stuff? Praise your child, say "Look at that, everything worked out this morning!" Pointing out your child's victories helps you to build their confidence.

**TIP #3:
Powerful Mantras Required Awareness

To create your mantra, power statement, or positive rant (see Tip #4) you need awareness. **With this tip you will want to catch** a "perpetual sameness" negative thought or negative criticism that you either hear yourself or someone else say and **flip the script! Turn the negative to the positive.**

For example, you catch yourself thinking or saying, "You're always late!" **Breathe and calm your emotions. There's no room for self-judgment, remember we're teaching our children by example.**

Then, flip the script to your positive mantra, for the whole day your mantra is: *"I am always in the right place at the right time."*

Here are some general mantras or power statements to get you started:

- *Everything always works out for me*
- *I expect great things to happen today*
- *I always do well on my tests*
- *It's so easy to make new friends*
- *Wow, homework is super easy*

**TIP #4:
Use a Rant to Shift Your Energy from the Negative to the Positive

My favorite brain training tip is a "rant." No, I'm not talking about a rant you go off on when someone cuts you off on the highway during rush hour. Remember your "magical matchmaker's" job? The RAS will match up whatever you keep thinking or talking about. Therefore, keep away from those negative rants. What I'm talking about is a positive "rant." A positive rant helps move you from lower thoughts and emotions to positive thoughts and emotions. I can't stress this point enough, feeling good first is key to improving any situation.

My daughter used a rant to overcome the jitters when she auditioned for the All-County Orchestra.

She was feeling nervous, so we started a little positive rant...

"Yeah, I'm nervous about my audition. I don't know what pieces they'll ask me to play. I don't know if I'll be any good, but I've been practicing each day and I usually play through the pieces without mistakes. Plus, my teacher told me my sight reading is spot on! I know this is new and scary, but I've tried new things before, and I did great! Like in gymnastics when I learned to do a *round-off back-handspring*; I survived that! And I DID IT! So, I can do this too! Yes, I play great and I'm going to rock this audition!"

That my friend is a brain trainer feel-good positive rant!!

**TIP #5:
How Using the Word "BUT" When Stringing Together Negative and Positive Thoughts Creates Powerful Shifts

The use of the word "but" between two thoughts, especially when creating a rant, is magical. Why is it magical? Because the word "but" negates anything you said before it. Your RAS only pays attention to the thoughts that come after the word "but."

In the above example of my daughter's rant, she used the word "but" to guide her RAS away from the negative thoughts, "this is new and scary" to what she wanted to focus on, "I've tried new things...I did great". This fun hack can flip negative thoughts to positive thoughts and will bring more positive experiences into our life. And isn't that the goal?

**TIP #6:
Intentional Action Is All About Feeling Good First

The last tip I would like to share is teaching your child about intentional action. How often do you find yourself in a power struggle with your child over doing tasks? Does your child stall when it comes time to sit down and do homework? Or refuse to clean their room when you ask them? If you're like me, it can be daily.

The brain trainer's motto is **"feel good first, then take action."** This approach results in more cooperation. It might sound simple, but it's a practice people are not taught! In fact, we usually expect our children to do just the opposite. Children are expected to get their work done before they can play. "Do your homework and get your chores done and THEN you can go outside and play!"

When it was time for my daughter to practice her viola, I was met with resistance. Instead of getting into that auto-pilot power struggle I used the "feel good first" approach. I suggested that she start by playing any song she liked to play on her viola and play it for pure enjoyment. After playing for fun, I notice she takes out her orchestra music, without being asked, and practices for her lesson. When it's time for homework I suggest we play a game or dance to her favorite music. Anything to get those feel-good vibes flowing! The tasks seem to move along smoother when my daughter is feeling good. Give it a try! At the very least you'll have some fun connecting with your child.

I hope these tips help you and your children discover how to use the power of your own brain to create more positive experiences and bring more joy into your lives!

CHAPTER SIX

It's All About Expectations

by Louisa Joy Dykstra

When I caught myself whining at my daughter, "Why can't you be more positive??" I had to stop in my tracks and laugh at myself.

That's what it looked like when I first started to apply brain training principles to interactions with my kids. I would exhort them to "Look for the positive!" or "You have to think about that differently or you'll never get anywhere!" It didn't take me very long to figure out that was not only counterproductive, but it was also just plain silly. When I finally realized that training my kids' brains had much more to do with me training my own brain before I interacted with them, things really smoothed out.

The first step is always being aware of your thoughts. So, when I would catch myself thinking something like "my daughter's room is always a mess," or " Will they ever become more responsible about monitoring their own homework?" I would stop and say to myself, Wait. That is NOT what I want more of in the future. Time for a different approach.

Now when I have those moments, I stop and make a mental list of all the ways my kids are amazing. They're so amazingly focused when they're doing the things they love. The more freedom I give them, the more responsible they become. When I see them as their best selves, the words that come out of my mouth, and my tone of voice, are completely different.

This plays out in an almost comical way in how the kids react to me, or to my husband, based on our expectations. My husband will say sometimes that the kids don't listen to him the way they listen to me, and of course we know the difference is not really in the kids. He and I are the variables; it's how the two of us say things differently. I am now pretty good at going into any interaction with them expecting a good outcome. If I'm asking them to fold their clean clothes or to unload the dishwasher, I know it will get done. If I must go back and remind them, I know it's just because they were really engrossed in what they were doing, so my reminders come out gently. The bottom line is the most important thing to me is that my kids and I are always on the same side. We have the same life goal: that they become happy, healthy adults.

It bears repeating – when I see them as their best selves, the energy I bring to our interactions enables them to show up that way.

The most powerful tool I have found, and I use it often when I catch myself, is what I affectionately call flipping *"the but"*. Here's an example. Compare how this feels:

I love you, but your messy room is driving me crazy! With how this feels:

I know I comment on the clothes on the floor of your room a lot, but I just wanted to remind you that I love you and you have so many strengths.

One starts with connection then erases it. The other creates connection. It's the same content but flipping which one came before the "but" makes a striking difference. Whatever comes before the "but" is negated, so put the "bad" stuff there, and the good stuff after.

I've learned that when I am worried about my kids' ability to do something, they can feel that in my body language, my tone of voice, and how my words come out. Of course, that affects their confidence. I'm getting better at catching my own thoughts before they pick up momentum. If I'm concerned about their inability to get a project done, nagging them only reinforces in their brain that they're not capable of completing it. Instead, I might ask what their plan is and if they want any help from me keeping focused. I'm happy to give reminders, but I always want them to feel we're in it together.

Does anyone else worry about what their kids eat? Obviously, a rhetorical question. What I most want is for my kids to listen to their own bodies and eat what makes them feel healthy and strong. That means I need to release my gripping thoughts and trust them. Because we're partners, I remind them to listen to their bodies – to stay hydrated, or to balance sugar with protein.

A very common area of struggle in a lot of households is screen time. Again, what I want most is for my kids to listen to their bodies and know what their brains can and can't handle. I use the "look into their eyes" test. When one of them has been playing a game or watching a video for a length of time, I have them look at me. If their eyes have a vacant look, I remind them it's time to take a break and walk around, look out the window, bounce a ball, pet the dog, talk to me, whatever works. It's been so cool to see them adopt that awareness for themselves.

Before I had kids, I thought it would be my job to "mold" them into good adults. But once I met my kids, I realized they were already wise little beings, and really, we are on an adventure together to help each other become the fullest versions of ourselves. We truly are in this together.

Suggested mantras:

- My kids have amazing positive qualities.
- My kids and I are in this together.
- My kids and I share the same goals.
- My kids are on their way to becoming happy, healthy adults!
- My kids and I enjoy life together!

CHAPTER SEVEN

Cultivating Independence

by Patricia Dawn Clark

Children bring many blessings, as well as challenges. Once you know what makes them tick, and how to help them manage their emotions, you'll have many more good days than challenging ones!

Your children come into this world fully dependent on you to meet all their needs. They are demanding and insistent. You learn their cues and your lives become entwined. Eventually, though, it's also possible to become dependent on their need for you.

As your children grow, they go through different stages of independence. When they are very young, the "terrible twos" and "threenager" years can be a real struggle. When they are older, the tween and teen years are a struggle of a different sort. Those are the days when you wonder, "Whatever happened to that sweet, loving, snuggly baby?"

Of course, you know they've done exactly what they're supposed to do! Your job as a parent is... to put yourself out of a job! You don't want your children to be dependent on you. You're just supposed to provide the nurturing environment your children need to explore and experiment with life in ways that aren't harmful to persons or property. I know this is hard; in fact, I truly believe the most challenging aspect of parenting is letting go of the belief that you oversee who your children become. You aren't.

Instead, you have the pleasure of discovering with them, who they are becoming. Not only that, but you have the gift of learning from them. Because your child already knows you intimately, they are an excellent teacher... about you! They quickly reveal to you the stories and triggers of past hurts all adults carry around, even when you think you're "over it".

One of the best gifts you can give your children is to train your brain as a parent. First, because it allows you to become independent and healthy in all your relationships, allowing you to be your best, unique self, living your own life. Second, because it's a terrific model for your children for how they, too, can live healthy, interdependent lives as they mature, grow up, and evolve through life.

How do you do this?

First, become aware of your thoughts, stories, beliefs, values, and priorities. Recognize that all feelings are normal and natural, but most people aren't self-aware enough to be able to identify and name them. Once you can identify a thought or feeling - "Woah, there I go again, jumping to the conclusion that he's late because he doesn't care!" - you can catch yourself. Pause… Wait… don't react right away. Think a better thought before you act.

When you do this regularly and take the time to explain to your children what you're doing, you'll be modeling this crucial self-awareness step for them to imitate.

Next, decide if you want that thought to continue to show up in your daily reality. What you think about does become true. The more you focus on the struggles and challenges you are experiencing with your children, the more struggles and challenges you will have. However, when you shift your focus to how amazing your children are. Witnessing the joy, they experience in every single moment of their lives. How beautiful it is to see them discovering new things. The more you will find joy and beauty with them.

Third, create a mantra that works for you to bring about your deepest desires and that excites you when you think of it. I heard a funny story about a woman who prayed, "God, grant me patience," and before she knew it, she had many challenges and obstacles where she needed to use patience. She kept looking for ways to use patience, which kept bringing her exactly that!

Even in my own life, my mantra for years was, "Every day, I am growing and learning," and I could pinpoint a moment in every day that I felt the struggle to grow and learn. The beauty of that mantra, though, was that I was able to shift my focus from the struggle to seeing the wonderful opportunity in growth. **My mantra changes based on whatever my deepest desire is now.** If you need help finding or deciding on a mantra, reach out or do a quick search on the internet. There are many out there!

Next, repeat the process. Post your mantra everywhere you will see it. Set an alarm on your phone throughout the day to remind you to take a break and say your mantra. Say your mantra as you are doing your daily care routines, such as brushing your teeth or driving to work. This will become a way of life for you, and your children will see this change. They will begin to have their own mantras. You could even create a family mantra together. Have fun with it!

You have the power to take charge of your relationships with your children. To recognize that they do depend on you for some things, but not on who they are as people. They are their own people. When they are still young, give them opportunities to try and fail, to learn and grow. So, when they are adults, it will not be so scary or difficult. While you cannot prevent all struggles in life, you can equip and prepare them to be mindful, intentional humans, contributing to the world in wonderful and unique ways.

CHAPTER EIGHT

Toddler in Turmoil:
How to Turn Moments of Madness into Magic

by Renee Realta

The journey across the chasm from cheerful and smiling to full whining took our five-year-old son less than two minutes. Forty-seven seconds later he was halfway into tantrum territory when I realized I was at the end of my rope already and my voice had started to rise. Somehow, I managed to catch myself just before I flew off the handle.

That was one of my better days. Maintaining control in the vicinity of a five-year-old volcano is never easy. However, I've had plenty of days when I've not only flown off the handle but probably broken it too. So, there I was, as time stood still for a second, pondering my next move. I thought to myself, "There has got to be a better way. It's utterly exhausting to correct his behavior all day long. Not only do I have nothing left in my tank by dinner time, but I also don't want to be remembered as 'that' mom who was always screaming at the kids."

By the time my son was a typical, emotional five-year-old, I'd been studying "brain training" for about a year and a half. Here I was, this almost-expert-level brain trainer and I was about to explode at my kid. That's when it hit me, I needed to change my mindset not only about myself, but about my kids too. Instead of expecting bad behavior, now that I was aware of it, I knew I had the power to change it. All I had to do was figure out what words I was repeating to myself and speaking out into the world that were causing me to attract this kind of behavior from him.

I put my mind on rewind for a minute and listened to the tape. Oh man. I had been repeating certain phrases out loud everyday like, "Why do you always do this? How come we have this issue every single morning? Why are you always whining?!" No wonder I was getting the behavior I didn't want. My thoughts and words were projecting the issues on our little five-year-old repeatedly every day, every time he wasn't behaving, and before he even had a chance to correct himself.

How was I going to handle this? This time, instead of escalating to the yelling stage, I started out by taking a deep breath. I closed my eyes and let my breath out slowly. Immediately, I felt calmer. I also felt more able to deal with the situation in a positive way... a way that I was consciously choosing. "Do you know why mommy is getting upset?" I asked. He continued to whine; I could tell he wasn't really listening to what I was asking. It was obvious he needed a little break too. I calmly picked him up and sat him down on a chair in the dining room. I told him he needed to sit there until he was able to sit calmly and quietly. Then I walked around the corner into the kitchen. It felt like forever, but within what was probably about five minutes, he was quiet.

Coming back into the room and sitting next to him I asked, "Honey, do you realize why I was upset?" He said yes, he knew why. So, I asked, "Why do you keep doing what you know isn't acceptable?" He replied, "I don't know Mommy."

"Do you like getting into trouble?" I asked. "No," he said. "Did you know you can avoid getting into trouble like this if you catch yourself and stop whining before you get so upset?" In that moment, I felt like I was talking to myself. We both needed that lesson. We both needed to remember to catch ourselves and take a deep breath to avoid challenging issues and bad behavior... or at least be able to work through them more easily. Ever since then, this is the approach I have tried to use with our five-year-old. Don't get me wrong, I still have my moments. As a parent, it's easy to get wrapped up in negative thoughts and forget that you hold the power to change things around within seconds. That's OK. I'm human. You're human.

I've learned, though, that becoming aware of my feelings and emotions is a habit I can practice and improve every day. I can acknowledge that I have the power to flip the switch and tell a different story, one that is positive. When I do this, not only does life become a little more peaceful, but our kids begin to learn how to control their own behavior and make better decisions for themselves. That's exactly what's been happening with our little man, as well as our teenage son, ever since we started brain training with them and brain training in our own lives.

CHAPTER NINE

Everybody LOVES Julian!
How to Make Self-Confidence an Unquestioned Fact in Your Child's Life

By Marion Solis

It was the summer of 2009, and I was attending my first weekend seminar for internet marketing. During the previous two days, I had been sitting through one sales pitch after another. This is not what I had been expecting, and I began to wonder if I had wasted my precious time and money (neither of which felt very abundant at the time). But then, something happened that would change how I parented for years and years to come... and it was worth more than any internet marketing strategy could have ever been. And to my surprise, this pearl of wisdom did not even come from any of the instructors.

I was sitting next to this young woman (I wish I could remember her name to thank her), and we got to talking about our kids. My son Julian was 3 at the time. She was sharing about her young nephew who had autism, and the challenges that came with him not feeling safe with people other than his parents.

I don't remember the boy's name, so let's just call him Tim. To make Tim feel safe, his parents came up with a brilliant idea. They created a book that had pictures of all the important people in this little boy's life: his grandparents, his nanny, his teacher…. Each page had a picture of that person, and then it said "This is Nana, and Nana loves Tim." "This is Grandpa, and Grandpa loves Tim." "This is Ms. Smith, and Ms. Smith loves Tim."

I absolutely loved this idea, and I decided to take it up a notch and into a slightly different direction: At that age, my son was still very shy and reserved, and I wanted him to feel safe. But I also wanted him to feel special and loved, and to grow up feeling confident and safe. I wanted to "train his brain" to expect that people love him. I didn't want him to grow up with anxiety about "stranger danger". What we focus on is what we attract, and I did not want him to grow up in fear. (And yes, of course I made sure he understood not to go with anyone he didn't know, but there are other ways to teach your child about "stranger danger" that do not involve scaring them to death.)

Instead of creating a picture book, we created a bedtime routine: After turning off the lights, we cuddled together, and I started listing everyone I could think of and said the following: "Let's say goodnight to everyone by thinking about them. Let's start with Daddy: Good night, Daddy! Daddy loves Julian. Everybody loves Julian! Good night, Omi (that's German for grandma). Omi loves Julian. Everybody loves Julian! Good night, Oma und Opa. Oma and Opa love Julian. Everybody loves Julian! Aunt Melissa loves Julian, Uncle Mark loves Julian - everybody loves Julian! Nana and Grandpa love Julian. Everybody loves Julian!

I went through all the members of our family first. Then I started listing our immediate neighbors, and later when he started school, I added his teachers and friends. Julian was not someone to fall asleep easily, so he heard the message "Everybody loves Julian" a lot.

If you are a little familiar with the way the brain works, you may already know this: your brain is most impressionable right after waking up and right before going to sleep. Whatever you feed your brain right before you go to sleep works on your subconscious mind all night. Therefore, it is so important to go to sleep with positive messages instead of negative thoughts and feelings. As you fall asleep, you can ask your subconscious mind to help you find a solution to a challenge you are facing, and often when you wake up, you have a solution. What you think about before you go to sleep is that powerful!

Your mind is also very impressionable right after you wake up. So, in the morning, when I woke up Julian, I reinforced the same message: "Good morning, Sunshine! This is going to be another amazing day! You are going to have so much fun! You are going to laugh and learn and run and play. I am so excited I get to spend this day with you. I love you so much. And so does everyone else - everybody loves Julian! In fact, your teachers and friends can hardly wait to see you!"

Especially if your child is still young, this is a great way to instill powerful, positive beliefs right from the very beginning. The younger your children, the more they still see you as "authority" and believe everything you say. **Use this to your child's advantage and feed them with beliefs that will serve them for life!** Even if you don't quite believe it yourself because of your own programming, if you say it with conviction, they will believe you. It will shape the way they see the world, the ways they perceive the world sees them, and truly embrace their vital role in it.

If your children are older, no worries, this still works - even when you have teenagers. In fact, as they get older, you can teach them to "train their brains" themselves. Then it simply becomes "auto-suggestion" (they feed themselves with powerful, positive messages). The reality is, you are always programming your brain, but it often happens by default, instead of with intention. Those default messages are rarely positive.

Think about this. If you instill positive messages into your child's brain every day - powerful, positive messages about their worth, value, and abilities - you will drown out the negative messages they are exposed to everywhere else, which can dramatically change their lives' trajectory.

Here are some of my favorite mantras to use with kids:

- Everybody loves you.
- You are a gift to the world.
- You are my favorite (if you have an only child).
- You matter.
- You are important!
- You've got this!
- You are loved!
- You know this! (Works especially well for test taking.)

There are literally hundreds of positive mantras you can use. Find a few that align with your values and use those again and again and again.

It is important to know that the intensity of the emotion has a direct effect on how the subconscious mind remembers these messages. So, infuse positive messages with positive feelings. If your kids aren't feeling positive in that moment, get them moving! Run, jump, sing, dance, tickle, laugh, PLAY... Do whatever it takes to move them out of negative emotions and into positive emotions. THEN the positive mantras will have a huge effect on their brains. As your children mature, teach them "auto-suggestion" (meaning they will do this themselves), because whatever we repeat consistently - infused with emotions - will be what we create in life.

At the time of this book's publication, Julian is 16 years old, and I am so grateful that he has a healthy sense of self-confidence and self-worth. This stuff works! And, definitely, do this for yourself as well - because everybody loves you, too!

PART TWO

AS WE BELIEVE, SO WE RECEIVE

*"Sugar and Spice
And Everything Nice,
That's what Little Girls are made of…*

*Frogs and Snails
And Puppy-Dog Tails,
That's what Little Boys are made of…"*

Traditional English Nursery Rhyme

CHAPTER TEN

Co-parenting with the Universe™!

By Murielle Fellous

I quite enjoyed being the "weird single mom" when my kids were growing up.

Even though they resisted all the coaching tools I tried to teach them, I quite enjoyed watching them turn around and use the very same tools and techniques to comfort their own friends.

They didn't always resist though. When it was important and something was bothering them, they did listen and tried the weird stuff from "Guru Mom" as they named me...

I remember a time when my daughter got strongly affected emotionally because of a teacher who seemed to really dislike her. You probably know the type. Maybe you had this teacher in elementary school, or it could have been in high school? Somewhere along the line, most people have had "that teacher... the mean one!"

If they weren't mean, they had favorite students, and it certainly wasn't you!

Whatever the reason was, you detested that class. This was when my daughter was about 8 years old. Every day she would come home from school very upset about something this teacher had said or done. Or because she had completely ignored her.

I knew that this lady was very judgmental and a discussion with her could have made things worse for my daughter. I also knew the one thing I wanted to avoid was for my children to grow up feeling like victims. I wanted to teach them that although they could not control other people, they still had power by choosing how they would react. They had the power, and the right, to refuse to allow anyone else to make them feel badly about themselves.

So, before I resolved to go see the teacher, I decided to conduct a little experiment.

I believe love is the most powerful force of all. Its impact has been documented and proven through experimentation. Because everything is energy, we can use the vibration of love to create the highest possible outcome. In many instances, even when we feel we are powerless to change something in the physical world, the power of thought through love and prayer transcends everything.

By doing so, the story we create for ourselves becomes an empowering one. We feel that we still have power, and we don't define ourselves as a powerless victim.

I explained to my daughter that when people are that bitter and mean they are often harder on themselves in their own mind, most of the time. It also often means that when they were children, they didn't receive the love and attention they deserved from their parents. I proposed to my daughter that we send love to the little girl inside her teacher.

We then sat down, closed our eyes, visualized her teacher as a little girl, and imagined ourselves hugging her and sending her love.

It changed everything regarding my daughter's experience. She felt like she was able to do something about her situation and that there was a higher purpose to what was happening.

Believe it or not, the next day she received her first praise from the teacher!

The stories we tell ourselves about who we are and how much power we have are creating how we see ourselves in the world, how we see the world, and how we see the world seeing us. Remember, the meaning you choose to assign to what is happening in your lives actually creates your reality.

When you teach your children to stop and reframe a situation or relationship, you teach them one of the most powerful approaches to life.

In fact, my children and I invented a game we often played on weekends or on road trips. The principle of the game is to take something negative that happens. Make up possible stories about what might have triggered this event and then, transform it into an experience of compassion.

One time we played this game when another driver cut me off on a Los Angeles freeway. We decided to invent stories about what could have been the possible reasons for his behavior. Here are some of the ideas we came up with:

- His wife is going to have a baby
- He is late for work, and this is the fifth time this week so he will be fired if he is late again, and he has children to feed.
- He is late for a doctor's appointment, and he will have to wait another month to reschedule if he misses it.
- He realized that he forgot to turn off the eggs he put on the stove and that they would explode when the water evaporates completely (which happened in our house once).

You will notice, none of these versions involves us nor has us taking it personally.

The lessons I modeled and practiced with my children were to show that you can never really know another person's story. Why do we create stories that don't serve our own happiness or peace of mind? Why not do the opposite positive? Teach your children to do the same thing. Empowering you, them, and others with whom they interact.

Cultivating the habit of not jumping to conclusions gives them the freedom to choose how they would rather feel.

Teaching them to practice that choice over and over will create the brain wiring that gives them an advantage for the rest of their lives. Enlisting the power of the "Universe/God/Love Vibration" creates miracles in their lives.

The best thing is, it is never too late, you can start now!

CHAPTER ELEVEN

Listening to Our Bodies Is Natural and Feels Good

by Patricia Dawn Clark

Over the last few years, one of the biggest and most impactful shifts I have made in my life has been to grow in self-awareness, both personally and as a parent. As I have learned to understand what makes me "tick" on the inside, I've seen a huge difference in the quality of my relationships.

The shift has occurred by paying attention to what's going on inside my body, both my thoughts and my feelings, and noticing how those internal experiences affect my relationships. I notice how each part of my body feels or pause to notice the thoughts I'm having; it feels a bit like I'm going inside my own body. That may feel a little strange when you first try this. You may notice aches and pains, or strong feelings you've tried to ignore for a long time.

Why is this important?

When you fly in an airplane, the flight attendants instruct you to put on your own oxygen mask first, before assisting others. This is great advice for most aspects of your life! The truth is, you can't give when you don't have anything left in your tank. You need to preserve your own mental well-being if you want to teach your children to do the same. It's important to listen to your body so you can begin to teach your children how to do it as well.

I remember when my youngest was first becoming aware of his body and the need for the toilet. There are many books and articles available that tell parents how to train their children. Train them in three days! Make a sticker chart. Give them candy each time they are successful at making it to the toilet. Setting a timer so you know to take them to the toilet very frequently, etc. But none of these felt respectful or self-aware to me. They all felt like a gimmick or a trick. What I most wanted was for my son to know how to listen to his own body. To first tell me so I could assist him and then to learn how to meet his own needs.

To be truthful, this was not a quick process. At first, I had to be extremely aware of his non-verbal cues. To notice when he was beginning to be uncomfortable. We spent all our time together, so this was easy. I was able to respond to his cues immediately. The more responsive I was, the more he was able to learn to recognize what was happening with his own body. After about a month, he was able to tell me what he needed and was ready for help at the toilet very consistently.

Learning to listen to your body will give you lots of information, from how to eat healthy foods to being able to manage your thoughts in a positive way. For instance, a fad diet doesn't set you up for success. Your body knows what it needs to be healthy and have energy. When you learn to listen to those cues, you will feel so much better! Teaching your children how to listen to their bodies will make them healthier and happier too.

The best advice I have ever received as a parent about ending food power struggles was the division of responsibility by Ellyn Satter (www.ellynsatterinstitute.org).

Your role is to provide what, when, and where your children are fed. Their role is to determine how much and whether to eat the foods offered.

This division of responsibility was so successful for our family, that I also started using it to teach our children how to sleep. First, I had to recognize that I am not able to control my child's sleep; I could only control their environment and daily routine. Together we learned when and where sleep or rest would happen.

Once I gave up control of the outcome, it was much easier and more peaceful to enjoy the process of creating a consistent rest routine. I used language and spoke with my infant about how we listen to our bodies. We are safe in our beds. We can relax and rest to recharge our bodies and brains for more play and learning to come. Stating what I wanted my children to learn - *"It is time to listen to our bodies and rest"* - helped them recognize the cues their bodies gave to unwind and relax. Yes, we did go through sleep regression phases and struggles, but it was not as stressful as it had been in the past. Knowing those are a natural part of the human journey was refreshing. I also discovered that I needed to listen to my own body. Naps became an item on my to-do list so I would also stay well-rested and ready to work later.

I encourage you to reclaim that fundamental human right. Make yourself a priority by learning to listen to your body. The more energy you have, the more you can give to others. Self-care is not selfish. It is the only way you can be empowered to parent the next generation of self-aware and mindful people. Listening to your body is natural and feels good.

CHAPTER TWELVE

Train the Parent It's All About Passion

by Tamara Jackson Clark

"Where are you from?" the Mechanic asked The Girl of the Wild Forest Light as he started maintenance on her swinging mast forklift in the Alaskan Arctic Warehouse where she worked.

"What answer do you want?" she said. "Where was I born? Where did I grow up? Or where do I live now?"

"Everything", he said matter-of-factly as he pulled up the forklift seat and swung back the battery cover under the seat to expose the battery bank hidden beneath.

"Well," she slowly started. "I live in the land of my wildest wilderness dreams on the Yukon River. To get to my home from Fairbanks, Alaska, I fly for an hour and a half on a small plane west over the wilds of Interior Alaska (where there are no roads) to a small village, and then from there, I either snow machine or boat 15 miles upriver to my home."

The Mechanic turned his head, wiggled his mustache a bit and looked at her with his squinty brown eyes. She could tell by the look on his face that her story wasn't one he had heard before.

"I am a Captain's daughter," she continued. "The ocean is in my family's blood and every summer, when I was a kid on Cape Cod, I would sail and swim like a fish, sometimes in jellyfish laden waters. I was a lucky kid with loving, caring parents and grandparents. But I always thought I was a little different. Even though I liked the ocean, I didn't feel super excited about it. I wasn't passionate about it. When I think of growing up now, I realize that the ocean was more of my dad's passion than my passion and that's probably something he may never truly understand."

The Girl of the Wild Forest Light paused and found herself wondering where the Mechanic was from and what his childhood was like. She wondered if he had kids, and especially, if he did, if they might be having similar experiences to hers, growing up? If she asked him, she knew he might talk instead of work, and she couldn't let him do that. So, she took a deep breath and continued…

"As a kid in my urban world what I really loved doing, even more than anything, was playing in my forest fantasy world under the trees and vines in my backyard. I would imagine that my favorite fantasy characters were there with me (Holly Hobby, Heidi, Caddie Woodlawn, and Anne of Green Gables) and we would play out our forest tales and adventures together. Even at elementary school, there were magical giant oak trees. The trees had huge acorns scattered all over the ground and each day at recess my best friend and I would race out of school, as fast as we could, to claim the best and biggest tree with the most amazing root system. It was there, in our fantastic magic tree world, that we would imagine a tree city with acorn people having all sorts of amazing tree adventures."

"There were so many forest worlds and wild places for my kid mind to discover back then that life was exciting. I had so much fun focusing on my forest passion. I LOVED thinking about my secret forest. I had passion in my life. I couldn't wait to get up in the morning to have my next forest fantasy adventure. Being a kid was FUN. There was so much to discover every day. And, most importantly, I felt good. But, like so many things on the road to becoming an adult, over time, I started to forget about my passion for the forest. And by the time I was about to start Junior High, my passion had almost completely disappeared."

The Mechanic had finished checking the batteries at this point and was just dropping the forklift seat down. As he started to grab his grease gun, he said, "So what? Why does it matter if you're passionate about anything in Junior High?"

"That's a really good question," The Girl of the Wild Forest Light replied, "I'm sorry that this is taking so long, I'm trying to get to that as fast as I can."

"Okay", the Mechanic sighed as he coated some grease on the front of the forklift mast, "Hurry up and tell me. I want to know soon before I have to go back to the shop, my twins go to Junior High next year."

"Really?" The Girl of the Wild Forest Light said in amazement. "That is so exciting! Junior High can be an incredible time of transition for kids if they know how to use their passion as a tool to Train their Brains. But, if they don't know how to do that, it can be one of the most difficult times in their lives and that's what happened to me."

The Girl of the Wild Forest Light sat down at her desk, then looked back up at the Mechanic with serious eyes as he finished greasing the forklift. "I was bullied by a few older girls in Junior High and because I was trapped in my own negative thought patterns, because I had lost my forest passion, and because I didn't know how to change the negative brain trap that I was in, I suffered all the way through 7th grade. Unfortunately," she continued, "I think that happens to a lot of kids."

"Oh," the Mechanic said as he started to put his tools away and get ready to leave the warehouse, "I'm so sorry to hear that. What can I do to help my kids have a positive 7th grade and not suffer through it like you did?"

"Well..." The Girl of the Wild Forest Light laughed as she walked the Mechanic to the door, "I thought you'd never ask. That is the easiest thing of all! First, they just need to learn how to be aware of their thoughts. Next, they need to understand how their thoughts are making them feel and, if they don't feel good because of what they are telling themselves in their own heads, they need to understand that it's easy to change what they're thinking so they can feel better.

Then, they need to learn to start talking about their current situation in a way that feels good. And, finally, they need to understand that they want to feel good more than anything else. They need to understand what their passion is and know that living their passion (no matter how different it is from everyone else's) will help them feel good. Living their passion will help them have fun and excitement in their day to day lives. Living their passion will transition challenging times to easier times and boring days to days full of opportunity and life. And that's it. Easy Can Be Zi."

As The Girl of the Wild Forest Light watched the Mechanic walk out to his truck in front of the setting Arctic sun, she noticed him reaching for his cell phone and she figured that he was about to call his twins to relay this Train Your Brain information to them as quickly as possible before he forgot. She was right.

Mantras

- It is so easy to feel good.
- Be a tree.
- I am a tree.
- I really like… (fill in the blank)
- I get super excited when I think about … (fill in the blank). Thinking about (enter what your child is passionate about) every day feels AWESOME!!! And feeling AWESOME makes me happy!!! And when I feel happy, everything is easier.
- Life is soooo fun!
- It's so easy.
- This is going to be a great day!

WooHoo, I love this stuff!

Figure 8: *Little Children Mantra Graphics by Tamara Jackson Clark*

Figure 9: *Little Children Mantra Graphic by Tamara Jackson Clark*

CHAPTER THIRTEEN

I See Nissans Everywhere!
The Secret to Noticing That 'What You Want' May Already Be Here

by Marion Solis

"I hardly ever see any Nissans anymore." said Julian, my then-12-year-old son, as we were sitting behind a Nissan at a red light on our way to school. His remark took me completely by surprise. Unlike many other boys, Julian had never shown any interest in cars. Quite frankly, I didn't even think he'd recognize a Nissan if he saw one - aside from seeing the emblem.

But as one who always takes advantage of an opportunity to teach and inspire, I immediately countered: "Well, neither have I, but I don't ever look for them either. Did you know that your brain will help you see what you want to see if you just tell it that it's important to you? How about we start an experiment called, 'I see Nissans everywhere', and then we'll see how quickly we start seeing Nissans all the time?" He agreed, and that's how our experiment got started.

Side note: If you have not yet read Deborah Owen's chapter 1 that explains how the brain works and how you can train your kids' brains, that would be a great chapter to read next. When I told Julian that our brains will help us see what's important to us, I was referring to the RAS - the reticular activating system in your brain. Here is an excerpt from chapter 1 where Deborah explains the RAS:

> *"Because the human brain is quite literally inundated with millions of bits of information every moment of the day, you would be completely overwhelmed and unable to function if there weren't a filter. This filter is called the reticular activating system or RAS. It's a network of neurons in your brain stem connecting your spinal cord, cerebrum, and cerebellum. The primary job of the RAS is to filter OUT all the extraneous information you don't need to pay attention to, and filter IN what you think is important."* (Owen, 2021)

Makes sense now? With our experiment "I see Nissans everywhere", my son and I were telling our brains that Nissans are important to us and therefore to filter them IN.

Now Back to the Car Ride

I knew I wouldn't be able to recognize a Nissan except for the emblem, and incidentally, the same was true for my son. So, I knew I was limited to identifying the cars in my immediate periphery while, of course, continuing to drive safely! There is a clear order of priority in my RAS, and "safety" ranks way above "Nissan".

Because I am also blessed to work from home - so am rarely out on the road - I was curious how quickly this was going to work. By the time we got to school, we had not seen a Nissan yet. I dropped off my kiddo, determined to see one before I got back home. And lo and behold, on the way home, there was one. I SAW A NISSAN! I was so excited! It works, it works!

When I picked up Julian after school, he had already forgotten about our conversation (no surprise), but since this was such a great opportunity to teach him how the brain works, I was determined to give this a few days. Well, on our way home we saw two Nissans, and now Julian was hooked, too. As we pulled into our driveway, I had to laugh: Our neighbors drive a Nissan, which is always parked in their driveway... and I had never noticed it was a Nissan. But since my RAS was set to look for Nissans, now I saw it.

After just a few days, we saw so many Nissans, Julian decided to change the game: now we were going to look for bright blue cars! And it didn't take but a couple of days, and we saw at least one, sometimes more, almost every time we were on the road.

We decided to up the ante one more time: Our new assignment for our RAS was: a bright blue NISSAN! Yup, let's see what's possible! This one turned out to be much more difficult than the first two experiments, and for days on end, we had no luck.

Then I took a little road trip to see a friend of mine, and I was sure that the one-hour drive would give me ample opportunity to see at least one bright blue Nissan. I got to my destination disappointed. Again, nothing. By this time, I was somewhat obsessed, I admit, and was seriously considering getting on Nissan's website to see if they even make bright blue cars (go ahead, laugh at me, I understand).

I visited with my friend, we said our goodbyes, I got into my car, pulled halfway out of my parking spot - and then I slammed on the brakes: there was a bright blue Nissan parked right smack next to me! I had to pull back in and take a picture for Julian. Woohoo, my RAS won again!

That was almost four years ago, and even though we haven't played this game in a long time, I still get excited when I see a Nissan, especially when it is bright blue.

Figure 10: *Marion's Blue Nissan the author photographed at the time of publication!*

So why do I tell you this story? Because you can teach your child to look for much more important things than cars! It is almost certain that what they want is already there... and then that's what their RAS shows them!

For example, if your child says, "Nobody likes me", you can bet that their RAS will show them all the kids that are mean or indifferent, because the RAS does not discriminate between "good and bad". If your child's attention is on "nobody likes me", that's all they can see because that's all their RAS will show them! But now you can teach your kid to say something like "I am so happy that I have some really amazing friends!". Of course, they won't believe it in the beginning because there is no proof yet. But encourage them to keep saying it and expecting that their RAS will find those kids that will turn out to be good friends, and they will show up! Just like the Nissans have always been there, so have the friends; your child just needs to know how to change the filter on their RAS!

Here are some other examples for how to use this, and then you can come up with those that are meaningful for your child:

- "I always have so much homework." turns into "I have so much fun in my free time!"

- "I am not good at sports" turns into "I am so excited I found a sport that's fun for me!"

- "My stupid little brother always takes my stuff" turns into "Look at the many times he respects my things."

Of course, you'll need to word it in a way that is appropriate for your child's age, so their RAS understands what it is supposed to filter in. But you get the idea. And now you can come up with fun ways to help your child literally create a new reality for themselves simply by changing the filter of their RAS. How cool is that?

And guess what? You can do the same for yourself! In fact, before you turn the page, take a minute. Give your RAS a project of what you want to see more of in your life. Repeat it often. Expect to find proof. Here are some ideas.

Be sure to use your own words:

- "I find more and more pockets of free time for myself!"
- "People love me and love to be around me!"
- "My kids are getting along better and better!"
- "Managing my money gets easier and easier, and somehow it just keeps on growing!"

Please do take a minute to create your statement now. You are worth it - and you just might be amazed how good it feels to repeat it even before you start seeing the proof.

CHAPTER FOURTEEN

...BUT!!! What If I Damage My Kid Forever!?!?!?

by Charity Nicole

Oops. I did it again. I yelled at my kid. See, I grew up in what my friend once called a "yelly family." It amuses me when I say "yelly family" aloud, because I've become conditioned to know that's the way we've always done it. I'm so used to yelling about everything, even when I'm not angry, that I never realized until recently this is a habit I should really work on.

As a mom, I want the best for my kid. I'm sure you do, too! And, as a witness of the mommy wars on the internet with lots of "judginess" going around, I've observed that even if some moms and dads don't agree how to do it, most of us wish to protect our children from harm and instill a sense of safety, security, high self-worth, and confidence.

What I've learned is that we get conditioned to repeat unhealthy behaviors as adults. Yelling is not inherently wrong, but it's a gateway to more anger. Angry outbursts derail us from being more patient, kinder, and to honestly listen to one another. Listening is a true sign of compassion.

It breaks my own heart after I lose my temper and yell at my toddler because I can see the hurt on his face, and I know I should've handled the situation better. The worst part about losing my temper and getting angry with my child wasn't the moment of anger, but the shame lingering in my psyche and body for hours, sometimes for days after. In those moments when you lose your patience and you feel like the worst parent on earth, I urge you to simply notice that thought. The thought that prompted the anger.

The worst part is that I vowed to be the perfect mom before I was even pregnant. I was gonna read every crunchy parenting book, watch all the documentaries, check out the swarm of great mom blogs on the interwebz so I'd be prepared for EVERYTHING. I never wanted my child to grow up feeling damaged - like I did - and I was determined to protect him from everything negative.

My parents did the best they could, and I know they intensely love me. But they couldn't protect me from everything. The things I experienced are the kinds of things no child should ever go through. It's taken my entire adult life to recover... and that's why, when I do yell at my kid, it hurts even more.

They were unable to protect me from sexual abuse or horrific bullying in school. Going through those experiences caused me to become ultra-vigilant about danger and risk. Every decision I have made since childhood goes through a rigorous assessment inside my brain to determine optimal outcomes.

I vowed that when I got pregnant one day, that child would be protected in every single way from everything... so that MY baby wouldn't have to endure the traumatic emotional states I experienced because of those ordeals.

I thought that if I researched enough stuff - GMOs, vaccines, nursing, co-sleeping, plant-based food, attach-ment parenting... you know, ALL the things... that my child would never go through anything traumatic and he'd have a perfect, fulfilled life. Even if he did end up going through a rough patch, he'd bounce back quickly because I took care to minimize all the other trauma.

Then, I HAD this baby. I went through my own periods of emotional desperation all over again. My 2-year-old son has tested me to my personal limits while simultaneously being the biggest joy I've ever known. In fact, I'm positive I forgot what joy WAS until I had my Valor.

However, with the uppermost highs of having a child also come lows. I vowed I would never be the mom who yelled at her kids. But lo and behold, I did. I've lost my temper on more than one occasion.

If I wasn't perfectly doing it better, then I was a failure and surely dooming my kid to a life of emotional instability, depression, rage and who-knows-what-else.

I told myself, "Maybe I wouldn't do these things if I hadn't been damaged myself." The thought of not being able to get it together, and passing down damage, was just too much to handle.

But one day, I discovered brain training. It finally dawned on me that my emotions didn't have to rule my life. I had been living on the mood roller coaster, topsy turvy from day to day, moment to moment, situation to situation, interaction to interaction.

I was constantly exhausted and upset and so angry at my Maker for allowing me to be a victim to all these horrible things. I truly felt hopeless and doomed.

When I realized that my thoughts dictate my emotions and it's always in my power every moment to turn my mood and personal experience around. My whole life felt bright. There was light coming through the crack in the door, and I finally realized that the trauma is a gift.

"A Gift" You Ask? Yes!

If I hadn't been through the experiences that shaped me, I wouldn't have this tremendous capacity for empathy and compassion, the desire to protect and persevere, to do good for others, to be a light, and have the drive to be better every day in every way.

I thought attempting to insulate my child from all things challenging was the only way to ensure he didn't end up a basket case like me.

Here's the truth: while I'll never be the perfect mom, I am genuinely doing my best. I take comfort in that because at the core of everything I do is the fact that the next day, I'll do even better. Worrying about being the perfect mom makes it so much harder to be a wonderful mom. Let's take that impossible pressure off your shoulders right now.

The best way to teach compassion, forgiveness, empathy, and drive is to be compassionate with yourself, forgive yourself and be driven to always do better the next day.

Every new day is an opportunity to be more amazing than you were yesterday.

The only way I can damage my child is when I stop the effort to model those positive behaviors and rest on complacency instead. I remind myself that everything will be okay… even when I make mistakes.

This message is for you too. If you believe it won't be okay, well, then you're telling yourself the lie that you are damaged forever and aren't capable of heal-ing. I know you would never want your child to think that about himself, so please don't believe it's true about you. You CAN heal and create a gorgeous, thriving life by training your brain.

In those moments when you lose your patience and you feel like the worst parent on the planet, I urge you to simply notice that thought. Be aware of how you're feeling. Take a few moments alone, even if you slip away to the bathroom to center. Decide then if this is how you want the rest of your day to go.

Your point of power is always in the present moment.

Right now, is when you decide that today is gonna be great. Make the decision that you're simply going to be with your child - with no expectations of yourself or him - and just say, *"We're gonna have an awesome rest of the day."* Say it to yourself over and over, about 25 times. And breathe. Then smile and join your child again and feel joy in the smallest ways together.

You are an amazing parent, teacher, friend. I know it, because you're here, reading this book. Be encouraged and know that your child not only has an amazing day ahead with you, but also an incredible life to live.

CHAPTER FIFTEEN

A Fable About Fear

by Tamara Jackson Clark

The Girl of the Wild Forest Light stood beside her snow machine at the edge of the frozen Yukon River and cupped her hands in front of her heart. It was late November, just after Thanksgiving, and at last she was heading home to the Yukon River Lodge. She felt such relief to be at the river in that moment. And that moment was the moment just before she and her husband, Sam, took off to travel the newly marked river trail 15 miles to the lodge. As she paused in her parka and heavy snow pants, scanning her surroundings, and taking it all in, time froze. And there in that moment, she started reflecting on the emotions she had felt every year for the last 10 years as she traveled over the newly marked trail for the first time each season.

Words began to float in front of her field of vision, words that described her emotions over the years at that moment: anxiety, awe, wonder, excitement, thrill, exhilaration, nervousness, calm and suddenly, a sense of FEAR struck her like a long, heavy ice pick dropping into the ice to chip out the first water hole of the season.

Her wild imagination began to spin out of control and started to take off like a Siberian husky who was jumping a fence at home in suburbia and was experiencing the thrill of running free for the first time. Her imagination was free and wild and even though she knew that Sam was an expert at checking the ice for thickness and making sure it was safe for them to travel, this sense of FEAR kept knocking, pulsing, and kicking at her heart. It wanted to run free like that Siberian husky.

"Emotions can be wild in the wilderness", she thought as a grin passed over her face and a spark of bright forest energy pulsed up through her body," I know how to change my emotions. I am a Brain Trainer. And I know I can transform my experiences just by the way I think about them. That gives me the control to transform this feeling of FEAR, this strong, overwhelming emotion of FEAR, into something else completely. I can change it into whatever I want, and I have some amazing, magic tools to help me do that!"

The Girl of the Wild Forest Light wiggled her fingers in her mittens and danced a little jig on the side of the river. She turned around in a circle to the right and then turned around the other way, grinning at Sam the whole time (who at this point thought she was a little bit crazy). She didn't care what he thought. She knew how to transform her experience from FEAR to EXCITEMENT and she was going to do it now! The first tool she'd already used was dancing to loosen up, relax and have some fun. The second tool she was getting ready to use was The Emotional Scale. And she had one more magic tool up her sleeve to use after that.

Everyone has a different way of learning, and everyone has a different way of putting into practice what they learn. It doesn't matter if you're a kid or an adult or a dog, it's the same thing.

The Girl of the Wild Forest Light is a visual, hands-on learner who loves to use her 5 senses (her sense of sight, sound, smell, touch, and taste) to help her learn new things and remember them easily. When she learned about 'The Emotional Scale' (see image below), she added a few things to help incorporate it into her life.

The Emotional Scale lays out the types of emotions you feel and shows you how to move from feeling the negative emotions on the left side of the scale (like FEAR), to feeling the more positive emotions on the right side of the scale (like JOY). As a parent, you can introduce this concept to your kids to make it easier for them to transform their negative emotions as well.

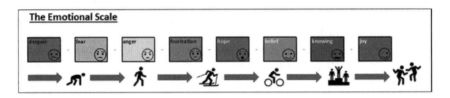

Figure 11: *The Emotional Scale and Rainbow Chakra Game by Tamara Jackson Clark*

Step 1 – Recognize where you are on the Emotional Scale right now.

Ask your child to pick an emotion face on the scale, or some words that would match the point on the scale where they think they are. Consider having a bag of color-coded words to match the chakra colors on the scale. Kids can pick the words that match where they are and follow the colors on the scale to pick out better words as they move from left to the right on the scale. If you write the words on small pieces of wood or plastic (almost magnet size), and put Velcro on the back, then put the other side of the Velcro stick on a cookie sheet with a hole in it, the kids can place the words on the cookie sheet and work with them, moving the words around as they transition, and taking them from the cookie sheet.

Step 2 - Think thoughts that are more positive than where you feel right now.

Use the words to help you describe where you are on the scale. Then use words that help you move to the right. That might look like this, "I know I'm kind of angry that I'm feeling any FEAR at all, and I'm frustrated that I'm feeling that way after all these years...BUT, I know Sam is an expert at getting us across the ice. He's done it many times before and today is no different than any other day. As I start to think about what's on the other side, I'm getting pretty darn EXCITED to get going again, and I'm ready to go! When we get on the Yukon River trail for the first time in the fall, it's going to be INCREDIBLE, AMAZING, and AWESOME!"

Step 3 - See the chakra color in your mind that matches where you are on the scale.

You and your kids can focus on the chakra colors to help you move and transition up the scale from the left to the right. The chakra colors are strong and positive, and they are the support system behind the scale, like your spine is the support system for your body. And you can add all sorts of senses based on the chakras as well, to move up the scale.

For instance, if you're feeling FEAR and you want to feel better, the chakra color that supports the beginning transition out of FEAR is Orange. Help your kids transition out of FEAR by not only thinking thoughts that are more positive but by focusing on activities related to the colors:

- Eat something orange, then yellow, then green
- Smell a mix or assembly line of orange, lemon, lime, and lavender essential oils
- Paint with orange paint, then green, then pink, all in a row
- Have a fingernail painting party, painting your fingernails colors that match the color transition you and your kids are making a reality

The Emotional Scale is a rainbow of Emotional Transition FUN! And it is something that can help kids understand what their feelings are and how to transform them in their daily lives.

Step 4 - Use your imagination.

Finally, there's one more tool that The Girl of the Wild Forest Light LOVES to use. It's her IMAGINATION!! And, especially, using her IMAGINATION to think about NATURE, and using the combination to help her move up the scale.

And that puts us on the edge of the Yukon River again where Sam and Tamara (The Girl of the Wild Forest Light) are about to take off by snow machine to travel home to the lodge…

Putting It All Together

SOOO…where were we? Here are the steps the Girl of the Wild Forest Light used to change how she was feeling:

- First, she was feeling some fear.

- After recognizing her fear, she danced a jig on the side of the frozen Yukon River

- She realized where she was on The Emotional Scale and thought about the chakra colors that supported the transition, she wanted to make to feel better about her trip home.

- She started to talk in a more positive way about her situation which made her feel better quickly.

- Finally, she brought out her favorite Nature Envisioning Tool (or some might call it her 'wild bird trick').

The Girl of the Wild Forest Light looked at her hands, which had fallen by her side, and raised them again so they were in front of her heart. Then, she closed her eyes, took three deep breaths in and out, and imagined a Magic Kingfisher lying in her hands. He was a plump, happy bird with shining feathers of brilliant blue and deep forest brown with a white rainbow pearl shimmering light swirling within them.

He looked at her with his wonderful, loving, compassionate eyes and leaned his beak in toward her. She knew how incredible and magical he was and thanked him for being there with her. And then, without saying a word, her Magic Kingfisher opened his beak and asked her to give him all the things that didn't feel right for her at that moment in time. He said, silently, that he would take them in his beak like he would carry a fish, deliver them back into the universe and then release them into the river to flow away forever. So that's what she did.

The Girl of the Wild Forest Light gave her Magic Kingfisher every bit of yuck she could find inside her and thanked him for his help. And when his beak was full (it didn't take long), she agreed to set him free. And that's where the fun really started.

The Girl of the Wild Forest Light loved this part the best; she could feel the positive, flowing, wonderful energy and excited expectation growing as she raised her arms a little higher in preparation to LAUNCH her Magic Kingfisher up into the sky. He gave her a nod with his shimmering head and the LAUNCH WAS A GO. With his beak full of yucky stuff, The Girl of the Wild Forest Light, raised her arms, bent her knees, and lifted her Kingfisher high into the sky as fast as she possibly could. He LAUNCHED up over the river and into the Universe where he burst into a Million Trillion little Magic Kingfisher sparkling pieces. And then, like diamonds falling as raindrops, all his little

Magical Kingfisher pieces dove through the Yukon River ice and released all her yuck, setting it free to flow downriver, never to be seen again.

The Girl of the Wild Forest Light opened her eyes and realized she was seeing the world differently. Colors were brighter and she had a glow in her heart and on her face that was not there before. She gave her husband a hug and a nod and got on the snow machine. They were going home, and it was AWESOME!!!

CHAPTER SIXTEEN

Little Eyes and Ears

By Deborah Helser

Figure 12: *Little Pitchers Have Big Ears by LACR*

When my friends and I entered a room with adults, this was often the way they greeted us, looking at each other with knowing looks.

It wasn't until much later in life that I understood the secret password adults used to clue in each other to stop talking about whatever they thought was inappropriate for us to hear.

In contrast, it seems as if all the filters have been turned off in today's world. As a parent, it's important to shield your little ones' ears and eyes from much of the information that spews itself from every angle in our technological world. (My mother used to say, "Deborah, with everything good there is something bad." That is true when it comes to the internet and cellphones!)

Before there were cellphones - ancient history, I know! - I had a chance to show my children what I was made of. The following is a true story and sometimes I, myself, wonder...did that really happen?

How Brain Training Probably Saved Our Lives

I believe it was the summer of 2000 (based on the ages of my children at the time of this occurrence, 10, 12, and 14), when we were heading home from a fun-filled (and exhausting) vacation at the CNE in Toronto, Canada. I was following along behind my brother-in-law, John's, vehicle in our Ford Taurus station wagon with our three children (my husband was unable to take time off from work to go with us which, as you will see, has a huge impact on the day's events). Keep in mind this was before most people had cell phones.

We had left our hotel room mid-morning, packing up all our belongings as well as filling our water bottles with fresh tap water. As we drove down the QEW highway on a beautiful sunny day, I asked one of the kids in the back to pass up a water bottle to quench my thirst. As I took a big gulp, I soon realized it was not my favorite taste. If you are used to well water and then must drink city water (lukewarm at that) yuck! I gagged on it, then put the top back on and returned it to the back seat!

We were nearing the "Peace Bridge", where we'd go through Customs/Border Security, when I noticed the distance between my car and my brother in-law's car was getting further and further apart, which made me wonder why is he speeding? Never did I think it was the other way around: why was I going so slow? Soon I realized the problem was mine, as I approached the bridge's incline, and everyone was passing me as if I was standing still! So, I placed our car in the "Trucker's Lane", as they were going at the speed of a snail just like we were.

At this point I was thinking I did not want to break down in a foreign country, as I did not know that my

AAA membership would work there (I later found out it would have). I also was VERY low on gas, thinking I'd save myself a few pennies since the gas prices in Canada at the time were way more than the U.S., even with the great exchange rate. So, with very little power (shifting my automatic from drive one to drive two), and very little gas, I proceeded to head over the bridge between the huge semis.

I started thinking a positive mantra in my head at this point… though I later found out from my kids that I was speaking it out loud! "Just a little further, we can do it, come on, you got this!" Over and over I repeatedly said my mantra whilst still shifting drive one to drive two.

All was going as well as could be expected in this type of situation until…the trucks ahead of me came to a halt. Hoping and praying for them to get moving just wasn't working. And while I believe in hope and prayers, at this moment in time I knew I was going to be forced to act.

I was now at a complete stop. Fortunately, because we'd made it to the crest of the bridge, at least we were on flat ground, otherwise what I was about to do would have never happened.

After vainly trying everything, I could think of to get our car to move forward, I decided to go ask the truck driver behind me if he could push our car with his big rig the rest of the way. I had it all planned out before I presented the idea to the man behind the wheel. I told him I was having a problem with my car - it wasn't going forward - and would he mind just pushing me until we reached the downward slope?

Unfortunately, he didn't see it my way. He said quite emphatically, "Lady, liability would have my head!" I then asked if he could radio ahead to the bridge authorities to let them know I was having trouble. He nodded and I headed back to deal with my three children, who were beyond worried.

In the short walk back to the motionless vehicle, I recalled a time while dating my husband, when his '72 Malibu had stalled. I had pushed him and his car so he could "pop the clutch" to get it started. That made me think if I could just get our car rolling and get it to that downslope, we'd be golden! My dad's words were never more important to me than in that moment, "Nothing to it but to do it, set your mind to it!"

When I got back to the car, I quickly told my then-14-year-old daughter, Tori, to slide into the driver's seat and listen to my instructions. Clearly afraid, she said, "No Mommy, no, I can't do this!" I of course told her, "Yes you can! I'll be with you all the way and all you need to do is put the brake on when I tell you to." Reluctantly, she slid behind the steering wheel as I placed my hands inside the frame of the open driver's side window. As I began pushing, I remembered once again my father's words, "Nothing to it but to do it, set your mind to it!" as well as the many times he taught us about leverage which could help him move just about anything.

Well, it worked! Whether it was the mantra of my father's words or the lesson in leverage, the broken-down, luggage- and child-filled car began moving forward. I'm not quite sure how far I had to push - the more you tell a story the bigger the fish gets! - but it seemed like it was at least 100 feet to get to the down slope. It took a huge effort for me to push that car! As it started to roll slowly down the bridge's sloped road, I told Tori to "move over, I'm coming in!" But there was a problem.

As I lifted the car door latch, I realized the door was locked! I was now running alongside the car yelling, "Open the door, OPEN THE DOOR!". Tori hit the unlock, I jumped in and immediately hit the brakes, leaving us inches away from the semi-truck ahead of us!

Now, I've never been the athletic type and have ALWAYS disliked running, so to say I was "winded" is an understatement. Gasping, I struggled to get the words out, but asked for that water that just a short time ago had made me gag. I took it and guzzled it as if it was a Perrier!

As I waited in the truck lane with my brake on, then off as needed - and still on the down slope - I saw a man on the left side of the bridge waving at me to come toward him. I shouted to him - in my head I gave him the name "Fred" (as in "Flintstone") - that I didn't have the power to cross the lane fast enough to avoid the traffic in the other lane. He stopped the traffic and instructed me to make my way (glide) to the side of a building where he was pointing.

I was headed to do just that when another man appeared - I called him "Barney" (as in "Rubble") - and was also waving me toward him. By this time though, my momentum was gone as I had stopped by the building Fred had instructed. I had no idea that this "new" waver, Barney, knew that I had no power and wanted me to use what was left of it to get into the Border Securities booth. I apologized and then Barney proceeded to push my car - along with Fred (mind you two of them as opposed to one of me) - into the area where border patrol asks you questions about your citizenship as well as your purpose for being in the country.

"All U.S. citizens?" the border agent asked. After each of us answered him individually he cleared us to go ahead.

I thanked him, then turned and asked Fred and Barney, "May we go now?" Fred and Barney said "Yes!" in unison and pushed us past the booths. Then Fred asked me to pop the hood so he could see what the problem might be. (It turned out to be a broken transmission!)

You may be asking, "What does this have to do with little eyes and ears? Or training your brain?"

My three children just witnessed their mother tackling a seemingly insurmountable problem, using lessons taught to her years earlier. Their little ears heard me repeat my father's words, and their little eyes watched how I managed one problem after another. Always remember that all you do or say is a lesson for your children! What kind of example are you setting for them? Good or bad they absorb it all. Be careful with your words and actions as they impact both your children and the generations to follow.

Oh, and two more things. First, if you were wondering, (as I was on that day), "Why didn't

Figure 13: *Counter-clockwise from Deborah and her husband (Wayne), Daughter (Victoria Amerine), son-in-law (Lee), son (William), son (W. Scott), grandson (Ethan), daughter in-law (Katie Stack) and granddaughter (Lily).*

*your sister and her husband stop when they didn't see you behind them anymore?" They told us later that they knew **I knew** my way home from there. After waiting for us once they got past the bridge, since there was no traffic coming across, they left. I told them, "THAT'S BECAUSE YOUR SISTER HAD THEM STOP IT FOR HER!"*

Figure 14: *Missing from the above photo are McKynlee and Raegan pictured here.*

Second, kudos to that trucker behind me who called ahead to the bridge authorities AND bumped his truck out to give me protection from the faster lane traffic only a few feet away. It did not go unnoticed. Sadly, however, it did go unthanked. Until now. Here. Publicly in this publication. Thank you to all the amazing men and women who take to the road every day. You are true "Road Warriors!"

CHAPTER SEVENTEEN

A Message for Your Child
From Superhero Hairy Thought-Buster!

by Michelle Lowbeer
Illustrated by Goran Vitanovic

Hello there! My name is Hairy Thought-Buster.

I'm a Superhero! I bet you've never read a book chapter written by a Superhero before!

But I'm not your regular sort of Superhero. I battle the bad guys people can't see – the negative thoughts inside children's minds.

You see, thoughts are tricky things. You can't see them, smell them, or touch them. And yet, they are very powerful. They color your body with different emotions, making you feel good or bad depending on what thought you are thinking!

My job is to bust the negative thoughts that make children feel sad, or bad, or mad. Because a lot of the time, those thoughts just aren't true. I call it STINKING THINKING. And those thoughts can last in a child's mind for a VERY LONG TIME if they're not taken care of. Some of those thoughts can turn into beliefs, which can last a whole life long.

But I'm going to let you in on a little secret: if you're having negative thoughts, you don't need me to bust them for you.   You see, you were born with a special gift - you can change your thoughts yourself. In fact, you're going to have to change them yourself, because I'm currently in Greenland busting "I'm not good enough" thoughts for approximately 2,158 children over there. (Brrrrr… it sure is chilly!)

So many people think that they are their thoughts! If they make a mistake they think "I'm a failure!" (Not true. Mistakes are just an opportunity to learn.) When they compare themselves to others they think "I'm not good enough!" (Not true. Everyone is ALWAYS good enough.) If they don't get the attention they are wanting, they think "I'm not important!" (Not true! Everyone is ALWAYS important!)

You are NOT your thoughts, and your thoughts aren't always true! So next time you have STINKING THINKING going on, you can say to yourself:

**"I'm not my thoughts, I am the boss
And I can choose any thoughts I want!"**

Here's how to change your thoughts:

Step 1: Become a thought-detective!! If you're feeling sad or bad or mad, figure out which thought is making you feel that way.

"Hmm... I'm feeling bad / sad / mad, I wonder - what's the thought I had?"

For example, if you're not able to do your math homework, you might feel bad because you're thinking the thought "I'm never going to be good at math." That's a thought many children think, but it's not a helpful thought at all.

Step 2: Bust the negative thought!

You can tell your thought:

**"I hear you thought, but I can't trust you!
I think that it is time to bust you!"**

Then, use your brilliant imagination to imagine me busting your negative thought! POOF!!!

Or you can say **"STOP!"** to your negative thought.

Or you can write your negative thought on a piece of paper and then, tear it up!

Step 3: Choose a thought that feels better.

You can tell your thought:

**"There's room for just one thought in my head,
I'm choosing a better-feeling thought instead!"**

Choose a thought that feels better. Say this new thought over and over again – until you DO feel better! In our example, you could say *"Even though I'm having trouble with my maths homework, I'm*

going to ask for help, and I am going to get better and better at maths!"

Step 4: Repeat as many times as you need.

If the negative thought comes back (which it sometimes will), that's OK. Just do steps 2 and 3 again. Eventually the negative thought will just disappear.

Easy peazy, lemon squeezy!

Remember:

**"Your thoughts aren't always true
So if you're feeling blue...
Find a better-feeling thought,
That's what you have to do!"**

I love you so much!

♥ ♥ ♥ Hairy Thought-Buster ♥ ♥ ♥

The Truth of You!

Greetings, human! We are the Fluffies.

We have descended from Planet Fluff to teach the children of your planet the truth of their being*.

We provide powerful visual cues that – with sufficient repetition and emotion – can prevent or eliminate limiting beliefs.

You are loved.

You are enough.

You are important.

You are unique.

THE TRUTH OF YOU!

You are worthy.

You are capable.

You are powerful!

You are creative.

You are OK, just the way you are.

You are never alone.

You belong here.

You are no better than anyone else, and no-one is better than you.

You are not broken. You were not a mistake or accident. There is nothing wrong with you. You are whole and complete and lovable, just the way you are.

❤ ❤ ❤ We love you so much!! ❤ ❤ ❤

The Fluffies

* Sometimes grown-ups like us too. That's OK. We love all humans unconditionally.

Download your free Fluffies affirmation poster to help children build positive self-esteem beliefs at https://hairythoughtbuster.com/!

CHAPTER EIGHTEEN

The Independent Thinker

by Constance J. Greer

At nineteen hours I'm Linda Blair from the Exorcist as they attempt to pry me off a nurse who dared suggest I wasn't trying hard enough. Then ten hours later, swearing like a sailor, I'm wheeled into the delivery room. Thirty minutes later a miracle is born, my daughter, the perfect gift... I'm in bliss.

One hour later, a nurse delivers Heather, my sweet girl, to my arms, and has the nerve to say, "Don't worry dearie, she'll find someone to love her."

Annnnd that was my first introduction to how people see a child born with a port wine stain. For those of you who don't know what that is, it's a dark birthmark that, in Heather's case, covered half of her face.

I'm looking at perfection, proof there is a God, and the only thing others could see was something wrong. Everything within me screamed, there is NOTHING WRONG with this child; she just has a port wine stain. I refused to raise my child as though she was "less than" and that was that. I had decided. I was resolute.

That was the easy part; the hard part was everything after that.

It was an easy decision; this mom was fierce, and I knew I would do whatever it took to protect this child. But could I teach her to think independently when the whole world saw her in a different light?

From that point on, everywhere we went strangers would look at my infant and ask,

"Hey, what's wrong with her face?" My response was always the same, "There's nothing wrong with her face. She has a port wine stain. I'd looked them straight in the eye, my voice even, just the facts.

Imbued with love, the tone was set, no big deal. Thus began Heather's unique brand of brain training.

At age two, we discovered Dumbo! "Fly Dumbo, Fly!"

Dumbo was different; he didn't fit in; he was made fun of it was lonely and hard. He became the hero of his own story, loved, and celebrated. We watched this movie over and over, singing all the songs, crying, and cheering every time! Dumbo became her mascot and the symbol of all things good and right about being different!

What a perfect reframe and new happy food for her unconscious. She slept with her stuffed Dumbo every night.

Later we're in the store again. Another stranger approaches, looking at my daughter and says, "Hey, what's wrong with her face?" "Nothing, she has a port wine stain." What's different this time is I can see my daughter out of the corner of my eye watching my response. I never deviated, I never got upset, and it was just the facts.

It wasn't enough that I was clear, my real job was to teach this child how to see herself, her real self and not be reliant upon the perceptions of others.

Three and a half years old Heather comes home from daycare and asks me if she is pretty. I said what a good question! Let's find out. I took her to the bathroom and stood her up on the vanity right next to the big mirror.

We lifted her hair and examined her birthmark. It covered half of her face, nose, cheek, forehead, neck and on into her scalp. It was even on her gums. It was fascinating. And then I asked her, "Well you tell me, are you pretty?" I watched her carefully and thoughtfully, looking at herself. I could see the gears turning, and then she turned to me and told me she was beautiful. I agreed with her assessment. And that was that.

Fast forward to first grade, Heather blows through the door crying home from school and locks herself in the bathroom. She won't come out; she's crying, and very, very upset. I'm camped next to the door, heart pounding, and going nowhere. I beg her to come out and talk to me. An hour later the door opens, it's dark now, and I pull her down and cradle her in my lap.

Through the tears, I get that there was a bully on the bus home from school who made fun of her. He was big, loud, mean, and made everyone stare at her face! Rocking her in my arms and telling her how much I loved her I proceeded to say the following.

"Did you know everyone has a birthmark? But for most people, it's on the inside. Everyone feels different; everyone has a tender spot inside. And did you know that only one person in ten thousand gets to have a port wine stain? That's right, you must be special! You are different. And now that you know what if feels like to be made fun of, you'll be able to understand how others feel when someone makes fun of them." I told her she must have a compassionate heart because - more than most - she knows what it feels like to be different. Then we spoke of the kid on the bus, the bully. She figured someone must have been mean to him, which meant his birthmark was on the inside.

This process took hours. I'm not sure how I managed to say all the right things except that I had made an irrevocable decision, in the beginning, so clearly there just wasn't anything within me to deny it. I would love and protect her, but more importantly, teach her how to think for herself.

As she grew up, the mascots for celebrating being different changed. In her teenage years, we found models that were famous because they didn't look like all the other girls. Lauren Hutton was one of our favorites with the big space between her two front teeth. Heather learned to play with makeup and was taught she always had a choice: she could cover it up or not. She chose to not cover up.

In grade school, she was the class princess. In high school, she was in theater singing and dancing her heart out. A straight-A student, she confidently stretched herself even when she was scared. She excelled in college and has had a very successful career in design, traveling all over the world. She is loved and respected. She is the one her siblings and friends go to for support and insight. And although she is human and expects much from herself, she always shows her real face wherever she goes. Without a doubt, she is one of the world's true beauties, both inside and out.

Figure 15: *Heather R. Black, the author's daughter, all grown up*

In summary: This beautiful girl learned through the early experiences with her birthmark how to think for herself, make decisions, set intentions, visualize positive outcomes, act, and keep her head on straight. Was it easy? No, it wasn't. But she has a mom who saw the truth of who she was and held onto that vision until she could do it for herself. Teaching a child how to think independently is one of the most powerful gifts you can give to them!

ABOUT THE AUTHORS

Angela Humburg

Angela Humburg is a Registered Dietitian Nutritionist and a Certified Intuitive Eating Counselor. After years of frustration with diet culture, Angela became The Diet Renegade.

Her passion is teaching others how to improve their relationships with both food and their bodies and becoming diet renegades themselves. She enjoys guiding clients in seeking their own unique body wisdom and rejecting diet culture. Much of her "education" has been firsthand with understanding and implementing the keys to brain training and body wisdom with her six children whom she has been raising with her husband Jeff for the past 20 years.

If you'd like more information about becoming a Diet Renegade, visit Angela at becomingadietrenegade.com! Super-charge your journey to Becoming a Diet Renegade in just 3 minutes a day watching virtual "flashcards"!

Experience Angela's Positive Prime session at https://www.positiveprime.com/dietrenegade

Scan the code above with your smartphone to see
a cool message from Angela.

Charity Nicole

Charity Nicole is the Princess of Positive Persuasion and your Funloving Leader at The #InstaHappyRich Life! "You can be happy and rich... instantly. Limitations don't define you!"

Charity is a Master Personality Marketer, Creative Heartist and Coach who pours her Sugarheart out through her live trainings, courses and written guides that teach you how to get your life together and have what you want (despite your circumstances,) be an irresistible influencer, win over the masses without manipulation and become a total social selling siren.

Charity can teach you how to do it ALL, because SHE has done it all: she makes pretty pics, purveys the truth through powerful discourse and is a total PRO at building fanciful fanclubs for life.

She has won awards for her work and been featured with many other top-notch internet influencers including Dana Wilde on her Time to Shine Summit, Train Your Brain U, the InstagramHer Summit and The WIFE Life.

Charity firmly believes you are adored, loved, and created with purpose, passion and a plan to BECOME the absolute BEST version of everything you dream! You were meant for more than mediocrity!

Check out what Charity's got going on over at www.CharityNicole.me: Take a class, grab a freebie or pop over to her free group and say bonjour!
https://www.facebook.com/groups/InstaHappyRichHQ/

Scan the code above with your smartphone to see a cool message from Charity.

Constance J. Greer

For the last 20 years, Constance has been an experienced leader with a demonstrated history of working in the professional training & coaching industry.

Her specialized skill set is in Coaching for Emotional Intelligence & Mindfulness, Business & Executive Coaching, Coaching for Parents. Speaker, Facilitator, and EFT (Emotional Freedom Technique) Master.

For more information, go to:

http://www.constancegreer.com/

Scan the code above with your smartphone to see a cool message from Constance.

Dana Wilde

Dana Wilde is an expert on how to change your mindset intentionally and systematically, so you get better outcomes. After growing her own business from zero to a million dollars a year in under 19 months, Dana now shows you how to make money by being happy and get paid for being YOU!

Dana is the trusted authority on fast business growth for entrepreneurs, particularly coaches, speakers, authors, energy and EFT practitioners, fitness professionals, and health and wellness entrepreneurs. With nearly 100,000 followers in 87 countries, Dana is the bestselling author of Train Your Brain and features in the movies, The Abundance Factor, The Truth About Prosperity, and Dream Big.

Fascinated by neuroscience and the power of the mind, she positively affects lives daily on the Positive Mindset for Entrepreneurs Podcast, where she reveals how to get clients, grow your following, and create consistent income by becoming the influencer in your niche and intentionally thinking wealthier, happier, and healthier thoughts. https://danawilde.com/

Scan the code above with your smartphone to see
a cool message from Dana.

Deborah Helser

Deborah Helser has worked 20 plus years as a Teacher's Aide with Special Needs Students as well as runs her own Direct Sales business with Pampered Chef since 2001.

She has been married to her husband Wayne since 1978 and has three grown (productive) offspring (Victoria Amerine, W. Scott & William) as well as a very dear daughter in-law (Katie Stack), 3-year-old grandson (Ethan), 17-month-old granddaughter (Lily), an amazing son-in-law (Lee), 8-year-old granddaughter (McKynlee) and 6-year-old granddaughter (Raegan).

You can connect with Deborah via her Pampered Chef website www.pamperedchef.biz/debhelser or via her email deborahhelser58@gmail.com

Scan the code above with your smartphone to see
a cool message from Deborah.

Deborah C. Owen

Deborah Owen is an award-winning public school educator, best-selling author, award-winning podcaster, copywriter, and personal and business coach. She is also a spiritual director (trinitarian theology), disciple of Jesus, disciplemaker, brain-trainer, and Enneagram coach.

She combines her unique background and experience to help her personal coaching and spiritual direction clients develop whole-person mental and spiritual health that dramatically and positively affects their relationships with God, with other people in their lives, and even with Self.

She works with churches to identify how to begin spirit-led disciple making that changes lives. And she works with non-profits to identify how understanding unique personalities can be a powerful force for collaboration and success.

You can reach Deborah Owen at Debbie@DeborahCOwen.com or visit her coaching and discipleship website at https://bookme.name/DeborahCOwen

You can join the Train Your Brain program at http://danawilde.com/op/train-your-brain-university/ or you can get the book at Train Your Brain by Dana Wilde. (Book link: https://amzn.to/2vDSdhV)

Scan the code above with your smartphone to see
a cool message from Deborah.

Kristin A. Carbone

Kristin A. Carbone is a heart centered Soulprenuer. She is celebrating 32 years of marriage to her loving husband Michael and is the mother of a fabulously independent teen named Makayla. She is lovingly sandwiched between caring for her daughter and her mother - 93 years young.

Kristin is passionate about self-care, organic living and helping women carve out time for themselves. Her motto is, "Self-care makes everything work!!" Kristin inspires busy moms and other caregivers to invest in themselves. She offers tips and tools to staying aligned in Mind, Body and Soul, taking them from Stuck to Spectacular!

You can visit her on her Facebook Page: My Organic Soul with Kristin A. Carbone, or reach out to her at: kristin.carbone33@gmail.com and receive a FREE Mindset Tool at www.myorganicsoulution.com Instagram @kristin_sharing

Scan the code above with your smartphone to see a cool message from Kristin.

Lee Collver-Richards

Lee is a versatile, engaging actor, author, and teacher with a creative spirit and exuberance in all manner of collaborative artistry and scientific discovery. She lives on California's Central Coast with her partner of nearly 40 years. She is a co-founder of the Melrose Avenue Magnet School in Los Angeles (2009); a research fellow of the Peace Academy of the Sciences and Arts in San Luis Obispo (2017); and curriculum designer for the SSS Ananda Van community school in northern India (2021).

She is a proponent of adopting a beginner's mindset toward all endeavors, creations, and the development of continual wonder, gratitude, and fierce compassionate stewardship for humanity's greatest teacher, the natural world, Planet Earth, Mother Gaia, now and consistently.

You can reach Lee through Mighty Networks' Conversations with Love, live the 11th and 22nd of every month at 11 a.m. Pacific Time.

Scan the code above with your smartphone to see
a cool message from Lee.

Louisa Joy Dykstra

Louisa Joy Dykstra is a mom, nana, rescue dog mom, business owner and author.

Learn more at www.LouisaJoy.com

Scan the code above with your smartphone to see a cool message from Louisa.

Marion Solis

Marion Solis is the Instigator of the "Being Yourself Rocks" movement where you can finally stop being everything to everyone else and start being yourself - because "Being Yourself Rocks"!

As an inspiring, heart-centered Mastermind Leader, Healer and Coach, she helps amazing people like you greet each day with "I love my life!" - and really mean it. Advanced Tapping (EFT), chakra-based transformational processes, and the five Life Purpose Profiles are just a few of the tools in her toolbox.

Marion loves to learn and teach. Her favorite tool to train your brain and supercharge your mantras in just 3 minutes a day is *Positive Prime.*

It is a simple, super powerful tool for both kids and adults. Try it for free at

https://www.positiveprime.com/?referralCode=yourock

To check out her other freebies, courses, and resources, come visit www.marionsolis.com.

She is excited to meet you!

Scan the code above with your smartphone to see
a cool message from Marion.

Michelle Lowbeer

Michelle Lowbeer is an assistant to Hairy Thought-Buster, a Superhero for young minds. Together they **write and post letters to children around the world** who are experiencing negative thoughts, a limited self-image or a challenging life situation. Through their letters, they **aim to create magical experiences** for children **which comfort them, make them laugh** and **empower them to change their internal narratives**. Woohooo!!

Michelle is also a children's book author, and studying to become a Biodanza facilitator for children. She lives with her two children, husband and cat Koala in Sydney Australia.

You can contact her at hello@hairythoughtbuster.com.

Scan the code above with your smartphone to see a cool message from Michelle.

Murielle Fellous

Born and raised in France, Murielle Fellous raised her three kids as a single mom in the United States for 24 years. She now resides in Tel Aviv, Israel with her youngest child.

Because of the challenges she personally underwent as a single parent, when her older children became teenagers and started acting out, she founded the "Co-Parenting with the Universe™" coaching and parenting approach and its corresponding podcast.

As an intuitive life-coach she is helping single moms with difficult teenagers prevent the downward spiraling into fear, overwhelm, guilt, powerlessness and/or depression. She's also teaching them to consciously co-parent with the Universe. Which means they are supported and always assisted and are never alone to face life's challenges.

A big portion of Murielle's work is based around emotional mastery and energy alignment using Clinical EFT/Tapping and a mind body and spirit approach. Connect with her at "Co-Parenting with the Universe™" https://www.coparentingwiththeuniverse.com/

Have a beautiful day, Love, Murielle Fellous

Scan the code above with your smart-phone to see
a cool message from Murielle.

Patricia Dawn Clark

Patricia Dawn Clark is a mother of four and passionate about the growth and development of our children in a respectful and mindful way.

Amid her mothering and educaring journey, Dawn discovered the unique personal and professional growth opportunity in direct sales.

Through her connections with Ruby Ribbon and Red Aspen, she helps women rediscover their self-care and confidence, signature style beauty indulgences, health and wellness, and their own growth opportunities.

You can reach Patricia Dawn Clark at pdawnc@gmail.com
Like and follow her at fb.me/pdawnclark
and @pdawnc on Instagram.

Scan the code above with your smartphone to see a cool message from Patricia.

Renee Realta

Renee is married and has two boys. She is a loving soccer mom and wife who's been navigating her way through life with creativity, self-discovery, and growth ever since she was young. She is tremendously passionate about inspiring people to believe in themselves. "It will all work out," has been a powerful mantra in her life ever since she became a single mother at the age of 22.

Having now overcome obstacles that could bring anyone to their breaking point, Renee has developed a mindset and strategies for succeeding no matter the circumstance. She has learned to pivot quickly and look for solutions and opportunities in every situation.

You can find and connect with Renee on Facebook and at www.ReneeRealta.com.

Media & Public Speaking Inquiries
admin@reneerealta.com

Scan the code above with your smartphone to see
a cool message from Renee.

Tamara Jackson Clark
"The Girl of the Wild Forest Light"

Tamara Jackson Clark (The Girl of the Wild Forest Light) is a Forest Reiki™ Intuitive Artist who lives a life of adventure in Alaska's wilderness.

She loves connecting people to nature, exploring the healing properties of trees, and is working toward publishing a children's book with her nature kaleidoscope images and the Forest tales that they inspire.

Follow her:
https://www.instagram.com/alaskawildinspiration/
https://m.facebook.com/AlaskaWildInspiration/

Scan the code above with your smartphone to see
a cool message from Tamara.

CONTRIBUTORS

 #1 International Bestselling author, speaker, & book publishing expert, Becky Norwood is CEO of Spotlight Publishing™. She is widely recognized for the empowering and intuitive way she guides others to weave storytelling into their books and marketing. She incorporates her methods with sound marketing that is the pathway for business expansion and audience growth.

Becky has brought over 300 authors to #1 bestseller. Through her Author Studio TV Show, countless listeners have heard her interviews of both authors and experts offering sage advice. She offers an extensive catalog of services supporting emerging and established authors.

Becky believes that a well-told story is a gateway for growth, sharing, and a way to unite humanity. She is an advocate for the positive that comes from sharing our creative genius and impacting our world in positive ways.

The Light for Spotlight stands for: Loving Influencers Growing Heartfelt Transformations

She can be reached at https://spotlightpublishing.pro

Sheng Vue, Book Website Designer

Sheng Vue is a Mother of four and a steward of new life. As a visionary and empath, Sheng is committed to creating a world free of pain and suffering through her strong connections to Spirit, her Hmong heritage, and to the revival of sustainable holistic practices worldwide, accessible to all.

Sheng is the founder of Niam Gaia. A star-hub of creations led by spiritual warriors and lightworkers bringing peace and ushering in right relations with our planet and each other. Each Niam Gaia contributor empowers Women, Children, and their Families as Stewards of Mother Earth.

In her spare time, Sheng enjoys her family, her husband and four children. Playing board games, reading, outdoors adventures, and learning from their environment. Sheng loves all genres of music, art, and books. She is a well-rounded, jack-of-all trades, Mother of many, and joyful contributor to society.

She can be reached at:

instagram.com/niamgaia/ or through her website: www.niamgaia.com

Martha Zimmerman Vorel, Book Cover Designer

Martha Vorel is the kind of person who gives so freely of her generous nature and highly intuitive and joyful personality. She is also a *Train Your Brain* alumna, and the designer of our beautiful book cover.

BIBLIOGRAPHY, REFERENCES, AND ADDITIONAL RESOURCES

Arlen, H. & Mercer, J (1944). Music and Lyrics for Ac-Cent-Tchu-Ate the Positive. Hollywood, CA, USA, Capitol Records.

Barkan, A. (2021). Democracy Now! August 13, 2021, Interview with Amy Goodman retrieved from https://www.democracynow.org/2021/8/13/not_going_quietly_documentary_film

Biskind, D. & Biskind, S. (2018). Codebreaker: Discover the password to unlock the best version of you. Marina Del Rey, California, Heart Power LLC.

Church, D. (2018). Mind to matter: The astonishing science of how your brain creates material reality. Carlsbad, California, Hay House Publishing.

Creed, L. & Masser, M. (1977). Music & Lyrics "I Believe the Children Are Our Future" New York, New York. Arista Records.

Descartes, R. (1637). Discourse on method. Retrieved from
https://www.britannica.com/topic/cogito-ergo-sum

Einstein, A (1942). A Letter to Cornelius Lanczos, 21 March 1942. AEA 15-294 ©The Albert Einstein Archives, The Hebrew University of Jerusalem.

Goodbaudy, T. (2012). The rebirth of mankind: Homo evolutis. PDZdzyn, Portland, Oregon.

Jung, C.G. (1959). The archetypes and the collective unconscious (Collected Works of C.G. Jung, Volume 9, Part 1). New York, New York, Princeton University Press.

Marx Hubbard, B. (2015). The evolutionary testament of co-creation: The promise will be kept. Los Angeles, California, Muse Harbor Publishing.

Marx Hubbard, B. (1998). Conscious evolution: Awakening the power of social potential. Novato, California, New World Library.

Resch, E & Tribole, E (2020). Intuitive eating: A revolutionary anti-diet approach. New York, New York, St. Martin's Essentials.

Satter, E. (1987). Child of mine: Feeding with love and good sense. Retrieved from
https://www.ellynsatterinstitute.org/who-we-are-2-2-2/#about

The Miracle Zone (2012). National Science Foundation 2005 study retrieved from
https://faithhopeandpsychology.wordpress.com/2012/03/02/80-of-thoughts-are-negative-95-are-repetitive/

Wallace, Dee (2021). Born: Giving birth to a new you. Cincinnati, OH, Briton Publishing.

Wilde, Dana (2013). Train your brain: How to build a million-dollar business in record time Bloomington, IN, Balboa Press: A Division of Hay House Publishers

ABOUT THE BOOK

"The authors of this book are parents who have been using Train Your Brain philosophies to raise centered, happy children and also to be happier and more centered themselves.

As you turn the pages of this book, you will discover that this book in not only about instilling a better mindset in your children, but also "training your own brain" too.

The best part of this book is that it far surpasses the original Train Your Brain philosophies because you get the combined experience of all the authors here.

These authors have their own modalities and techniques woven into their parenting experience, alongside Train Your Brain.

You have in your hands a tome of wisdom that will inspire you and benefit your children. It's a book that couldn't have been created any other way."

— Dana Wilde
Author of *Train Your Brain: How to Build a Million Dollar Business in Record Time* and creator of *The Mind Aware* and many get-the-job-done-with-joy-and-ease programs.

WE LOVE REVIEWS!

If you have read this book and resonated with the contents we would so appreciate your feedback.

Simply go to the site you purchased the book from to leave your review.

A warm THANK YOU from all of the Authors!

Made in the USA
Columbia, SC
27 April 2024